"If honest worship is a matter of remaining unhidden in the presence of God, living without pretenses before a watching world, and being ruthlessly committed to truthful self-examination, then that is the kind of worship the church sorely needs, even if it is awfully difficult to achieve. By God's grace it is achievable. Helps are needed though, and this book is precisely the kind of help that gets pastors and parishioners worshiping honestly before a gracious God, for whom such worship is deeply pleasing."

W. David O. Taylor, Fuller Theological Seminary

"You had me at 'why do we need smoke machines in church?'! *Honest Worship* is a must-read for anyone who is involved in leading or participating in worship. It is honest, challenging, convicting, and inspiring—and it will change the way you approach this key, spiritual practice!"

Ruth Haley Barton, founding president/CEO at Transforming Center, author of *Life Together in Christ*

"As both an artist and a worship leader, I highly recommend this book by my friend, Manuel Luz. It's a wonderful invitation for each of us to engage wholeheartedly in authentic worship beyond all the trappings that so easily entangle us. These are wise words from a seasoned leader in the arts and worship who knows the difference between trends and truth. Well done!"

Matt Tommey, artist, author, and worship leader

"We all worship something, whether we realize it or not. If you've chosen to worship God, you need this book. If you lead others in worship of God, you need this book. It will open your eyes to what has been missing in our worship. *Honest Worship* shows us how to really align our souls with the One who made us so that we can experience the fullness of worshiping 'in spirit and truth.'"

J. Scott McElroy, author *Creative Church Handbook* and *Finding Divine Inspiration*

"Dallas Willard was fond of saying that worship should be understood as properly ascribing worth to God. This work helps readers understand how and why we must endeavor to do that very thing. Our humanity depends on it."

Gary Black Jr., Azusa Pacific University

"I first met Manuel Luz a couple of decades ago, and have watched his own worship journey from a distance. This book is the fruit of that long journey. Manuel provides a thoughtful framework for looking at the big picture of what it means to worship our God with honesty, obedience, devotion, and passion. I highly recommend this for every individual who longs to grow in worship, and for every leader who is guiding others into God's presence."

Nancy Beach, leadership coach with Slingshot Group, author of *An Hour on Sunday*

"Over the past twenty years I have spent many hours with Manuel neck deep in the unspectacular details of everyday church life and ministry. From the front row, I have watched him pour himself out in sacrificial and tireless service to God, our staff, our congregation, and people all over the world.... This book is the product of God's Spirit doing genuine soul work in a man willing to cooperate, stretch, and grow. Our preference for inauthenticity is one of the reasons the church is now in so much trouble. We desperately need *Honest Worship*. Today, because of the narrow road Manuel has traveled, he is the best person to have written this exceptional book."

Mike Lueken, senior pastor of Oak Hills Church in Folsom, California, coauthor of *Renovation of the Church*

HONEST
WORSHIP

FROM FALSE SELF TO TRUE PRAISE

Manuel Luz

FOREWORD BY RORY NOLAND

IVP Books

An imprint of InterVarsity Press
Downers Grove, Illinois

InterVarsity Press
P.O. Box 1400, Downers Grove, IL 60515-1426
ivpress.com
email@ivpress.com

Cover design: Cindy Kiple
Interior design: Jeanna Wiggins
cover image: colorful abstract smoke: © Thomas Vogel/iStockphoto

ISBN 978-0-8308-4538-5 (print)
ISBN 978-0-8308-8025-6 (digital)

Printed in the United States of America ♾

Library of Congress Cataloging-in-Publication Data
Names: Luz, Manuel, author.
Title: Honest worship : from false self to true praise / Manuel Luz ;
  foreword by Rory Noland.
Description: Downers Grove : InterVarsity Press, 2018. | Includes
  bibliographical references.
Identifiers: LCCN 2018014459 (print) | LCCN 2018021732 (ebook) | ISBN
  9780830880256 (eBook) | ISBN 9780830845385 (pbk. : alk. paper)
Subjects: LCSH: Worship. | Spirituality—Christianity.
Classification: LCC BV10.3 (ebook) | LCC BV10.3 .L89 2018 (print) | DDC
  264—dc23
LC record available at https://lccn.loc.gov/2018014459

P	21	20	19	18	17	16	15	14	13	12	11	10	9	8	7	6	5	4	3	2
Y	35	34	33	32	31	30	29	28	27	26	25	24	23	22	21	20	19	18

CONTENTS

FOREWORD

Rory Noland

WHEN PAUL URGES BELIEVERS to offer their bodies as living sacrifices and juxtaposes this definition of "true and proper worship" with an invitation to be transformed by the renewing of our minds, he is underscoring the interdependent relationship between worship and spiritual formation (Romans 12:1-2). Simply put, worship can be spiritually formative, and those who attend to their ongoing spiritual growth inevitably become vibrant worshipers.

Though much is being written today on worship and spiritual formation as separate studies, Manuel Luz skillfully details the relationship between the two in his aptly titled book, *Honest Worship*. As an experienced practitioner in the fields of both worship and spiritual formation, Manuel offers biblical insights and sound advice gleaned from his own personal experience. His writing reflects his depth of character, his intimate walk with the Lord, and his sensitive, shepherd's heart—all traits I've admired in Manuel since we met three decades ago.

In the following pages, my friend not only describes honest worship as emanating from the depths of one's soul, but provides practical guidance on how to realize such transcendent worship in our lives. Each chapter probes a different issue related to the false self—such as narcissism and pride—that hinders us from worshiping God from our true selves, which is the fullest expression of who God made us to be.

I encourage you to read this book slowly and prayerfully and to interact with the spiritual practices offered at the end of every chapter. Take the contents of each section deep into your soul. In other words, allow the wisdom of this book to renew your mind and free you up to worship the Lord from your true self.

PREFACE

I DIDN'T ORIGINALLY INTEND TO WRITE a book on worship. And I had many seemingly legitimate justifications for not doing so. All of the really good books on worship had already been written by many brilliant and godly people over the centuries, I reasoned. What knowledge could I impart, what experience could I share, what teaching could I instill that could possibly be unique and relevant and insightful? And what amount of spiritual arrogance might I have to think I could write a book on something so hallowed and near to the heart of God? It felt a bit presumptuous, complicated, daunting.

But there was this stirring. Perhaps it was a holy discomfiture I sometimes felt when experiencing certain strains of worship, a wiggle in my soul compass that suggested we weren't always headed true north. Certainly there are forces—both cultural and within the church—that we must be mindful of. Perhaps it was simply the awareness that people were settling for worship instead of diving into the deeper waters. Because it truly is my hope that people experience more fully orbed worship—in their corporate expression, in their theology and practices, and lived out from their souls. Or perhaps it was a feeling in my gut that I just didn't want to pretend anymore—to myself and to my God—

and there were cloudy, subterranean aspects of my identity that I still needed to disempower and lay down in order to become the worshiper God intended me to be.

But the stirring wasn't foundationally an issue of music or style or approach, not even of what was happening on the stage. It was not in the superficialities that often drive conversations about worship. It had more to do with how God had been transforming me over the course of my life. It had more to do with my spiritual formation and how my continuing sanctification deepened not only my relationship with God but my worship of him. As I became more and more formed—spiritually, psychologically, theologically, soulfully—worship was becoming more and more the language of who I was before God.

This book is an attempt to bring together some thoughts and concepts in spiritual formation with the current state of the art in worship. With this in mind, I deal with external issues such as cultural narcissism, high-tech trendiness, and consumerism and how they have infiltrated our worship. I address internal issues such as personal identity, false self, ambition, and pride and emphasize the importance of understanding the truth of who we are so that we might worship more fully. I try to deconstruct our preconceptions of the soul and apply a fuller understanding to my favorite definition of worship—to love the Lord God with heart and mind and strength. And I discuss corporate worship issues such as what it means to more deeply embrace biblical community, God's metanarrative story, and the sabbath.

I'm guessing that you're probably reading this because of the title of this book. So what do we mean when we say *honest worship*? To ask this is to invite the reader beyond the deep waters of who you think you are, and possibly who you pretend to be, in order to come before our loving and gracious God as you truly are.

Honest worship is worship that is not tainted by the stylistic preferences and vanities of our false selves, nor clouded by the cultural forces of narcissism or consumerism or spectacle, but instead comes from our true selves before our holy God. Honest worship is worship that emanates from the depth of your entire soul—your will, intellect, passions, emotions, and body all aligned to the will of God. Honest worship is living the entirety of your life in a way that is increasingly more abandoned to giving God glory, not only on Sundays but on every day of the week. And honest worship is worship that extends beyond yourself to love and care for others, to be an instrument for justice and redemption and peace.

Ultimately, I hope this book carefully and sensitively encourages the worshiper to come before God—humbly and hopefully—with sandals off, as if we are on holy ground.

Because we are.

One

HOLY SMOKE

> Then he was told, "Go, stand on the mountain
> at attention before GOD. GOD will pass by."
>
> A hurricane wind ripped through the mountains
> and shattered the rocks before GOD, but GOD
> wasn't to be found in the wind; after the wind an
> earthquake, but GOD wasn't in the earthquake; and
> after the earthquake fire, but GOD wasn't in the fire;
> and after the fire a gentle and quiet whisper.
>
> When Elijah heard the quiet voice, he muffled
> his face with his great cloak, went to the
> mouth of the cave, and stood there.
>
> **1 KINGS 19:11-13** *THE MESSAGE*

MY TEENAGE SON, JUSTIN, had been invited to an area church by a friend. Since he had grown up as a PK (pastor's kid) and had never been to a megachurch like this before, I wondered what impression it might give him.

Sure enough, soon after his experience, Justin asked me a question: "Why do they need smoke machines in church?"

There was much I could have said in that moment. I could have contrasted different philosophies of ministry, especially in relation to the seeker movement in our postmodern culture, and explained how some view the Sunday service as having components of both worship and evangelism. I could have articulated the differences between entertainment and engagement and how the two, while they may look similar, are very different in intent and outcome. And I could have passionately shared my deeply held convictions on worship theology, what it means to come before the throne of God as the people of God, the bride and the Bridegroom, the community of believers with the community of the Godhead. But I didn't.

Instead I simply replied, "Well, technically, you need the smoke machines to be able to see the lasers."

THE STATE OF THE ART

Generalizing broadly, worship in a number of churches today is a far cry from that of previous generations. Computer-controlled concert lighting, digital automated sound systems, high decibels, and high-definition screens create a dynamic, multisensory experience. On the expansive platform, talented musicians command center stage, performing the current worship songs with note-for-note perfection, underscored by click tracks and drum loops. Ushers greet people warmly, offering ear plugs along with the bulletins. There's an emphasis on branding, social media, and corporate organization. There may even be a hipster self-awareness that permeates the room, an anti-fashion fashionableness.

These churches, which some refer to as "attractional model," carefully and purposefully design high-impact experiences to attract people to their weekend services. With roots that trace through the seeker movement of the eighties and nineties, they understand that high production values and marquee personalities both attract nonbelievers and retain believers. High-tech media and pop style are the vernacular of modern culture and can be used to effectively speak into that culture. And to these churches' credit, many people come and worship God, mature as Christians, and share their faith.

Smaller churches, which often sit in the shadows of their neighboring megachurches, are also swept into the slipstream of this cutting edge. Small and medium-sized churches are often caught in the whirlwind of trying to modernize technology, media, facilities, web presence—and talent. Even volunteer worship leaders feel the pressure to "sound like the record" when they lead worship.

Due to the explosion of the worship industry in the last decade (from CDs to radio airplay to major concert tours), musical selection in worship services has become more important than ever. People want to hear their latest favorite worship songs. And while the worship wars of the previous generation are generally a distant memory, we are still jounced by their wake. Hymn books, pipe organs, and choirs have become anachronisms. Some churches have settled on separate services, providing traditional and blended alternatives. While this pragmatism has proved workable for many churches, the issue remains that worship has too often devolved into stylistic preferences.

In the midst of these sweeping trends, some attenders succumb to the temptation to church-hop, sampling church services like so many downtown restaurants. Many older attenders are unsettled, even exasperated by the changes, and make it their business to rally for some semblance of familiarity, for hymns and "praise choruses." Some young and old, unimpressed by the high production values of today's churches, are instead turning to liturgy, to quieter, ancient-future expressions of the faith, in order to meet an unhurried God.[1] Others, seeking more organic community, are attending intimate, high-touch house churches. But the disturbing trend is that some people—from boomers to millennials—are choosing to leave the institution of the church entirely. Perhaps they have been jaded by the experience of church or the attitudes of the attenders, like Dorothy discovering the wizard behind the curtain. Or perhaps the world's distractions are simply too big and too loud to ignore.

Certainly the church is in flux. And the implications for worship—and the worshiper—are many.

Now, I'm not doubting the sincerity or integrity of any of these churches or of their leaders. I firmly believe that these churches are filled with good-hearted, God-focused people who are trying to do their best to further the kingdom. I also don't have anything against high-tech production or hip music or excellence in the arts. Cutting-edge worship music is a staple at the church I pastor, and for many years I've been an outspoken advocate for the arts in the church and for artists of faith. This is an exciting time to be an artist of faith, and I'm grateful to be a part of it all. Further, I have many friends and associates who minister in both small churches and megachurches, and I know them to be God-honoring Christ-followers. But there are pitfalls and tripwires all around these issues of which we must be acutely aware. As A. W. Tozer warned, "Worship is no longer worship when it reflects the culture around us more than the Christ within us."[2]

At the crux of all these trends is the desire to help worshipers worship, to meet God in a transcendent and transformative way, and to give God glory. And that's a good thing. The holes in our hearts can be filled only by God, and it is the calling of the church to help people become heart-filled and soul-alive.

SPECTACLE AND TRANSCENDENCE

As humans, we long for transcendence.[3] We long for experiences that take us beyond the mere material, corporeal world. We thirst for things beyond this earthly plane, things that lift us up and give us a sense of wholeness and acceptance and assurance. We were made this way. This universal longing is a good thing because it serves as a divining rod of sorts, pointing us to the one true God.

But we are self-focused beings by nature, living in an increasingly narcissistic culture. And we take that cultural self-centeredness into our worship services in deep and subversive ways that we may not realize. We bring our angst, our neediness, our consumer-driven worldview, our pop-culture appetites, and our narcissistic tendencies into Sunday morning. Instead of seeking communion with God, we often seek experiences of God. Instead of encounter, we settle for escapism. When we do, we're in danger of revering the experience more than the Person. And that puts us in a precarious place.

Transcendent moments with God can't be manufactured. No matter how we try, we can't program them, design them, or will them to happen. Transcendence is a Holy Spirit thing.

So we turn to the arts, which are transcendent in nature. They can express the unexplainable and convey emotion, beauty, and truth beyond mere words. Using the arts, we create spectacle, because that's what we know how to do. We compose amazing songs and assemble talented bands with accomplished vocalists to sing them. We employ mind-blowing sound, lighting, and multimedia systems. We incorporate theatrical and visual arts into our productions. Whether it be a mass choir and orchestra, a rock band with pulsing lasers, or a gospel fusion ensemble with a horn section, we create emotive and sensational experiences. Because we're human beings and because the arts are a natural part of how we express ourselves, we create great spectacles. And honestly, we're really good at it. We've become quite sophisticated at stirring our emotions and impressing ourselves. But spectacle can turn people into spectators. And the act of worship is neither passive nor inert.

Now, I'm not saying that God-breathed transcendence doesn't happen in these experiences. It most certainly does. What I am saying is that we're sometimes too quick to create spectacle, too quick to want to be wowed and have our emotions stirred in the name of God. If we are brutally honest with ourselves, we will admit this to be too often true. We can't manufacture holy transcendence, but we can manufacture spectacle, so we create spectacular services that titillate and tease, inspire and impress. And then we trust that God will show up.

I know this to be true—because I am one of those leaders who created spectacle, who led large teams of musicians, artists, and technicians to create grand and glorious shows brimming with the gospel, full of great energy and creativity and technology. It was my job. We did it really well. And truth be told, we were all a little intoxicated by the thrill of it.

HOLY SMOKE

Of course, the author of true transcendence is the Holy Spirit. And in worship, both personal and corporate, the Spirit is where we should begin and end. In his conversation with the Samaritan woman, Jesus patiently offered her this correction as it related to worship: "A time is coming and has now come when the true worshipers will worship the Father in the Spirit and in truth, for they are the kind of worshipers the Father seeks. God is spirit, and his worshipers must worship in the Spirit and in truth" (John 4:23-24).

During this interchange, Jesus repeated the phrase "in the Spirit and in truth." He emphasized the Spirit, because the Spirit authenticates true worship. Worship happens in the communing of our spirits with the Holy Spirit. He also emphasized truth, in part because he was contrasting Jewish worship, which pointed to the one true God, to Samaritan worship, which pointed to "what you do not know" (John 4:22).

Worship is dialogical, a continuing interaction of revelation and response. Constance Cherry writes, "God's action invites a response. God's initiatives always result in an invitation to trust God and respond to and receive the action offered. This engagement of revelation/response forms the core of Christian worship."[4] God reveals himself to us when we gather, and then we respond to that revelation with external actions, such as singing and exaltation, and with internal actions, such as repentance and reverence. This continuing revelation and response is done in the presence of—and I would say is *driven by*—the Spirit of God. The Spirit moves in us to reveal, revive, convict, assure, comfort, admonish, and inspire. God-centered worship is permeated by the Spirit. This is what it is to worship in the Spirit.

The Spirit helps us to see beyond the material world—into the holy transcendence—and helps to bring us before the throne. James B. Torrance offers this more complete view of worship: "As in worship, so also in our personal relationships with one another, we are given the gift of participating through the Spirit in the incarnate Son's communion with the Father, in the Trinitarian life of God."[5] This is the wondrous relational essence of worship: the community of the Trinity calling and communing with the community of his people.

Here is my fear for the church: in the midst of all the smoke machines, high-def video loops, and latest worship hits, we may be settling for something less than true transcendence, something less than Spirit-breathed worship, something less than God on God's terms. Are we inadvertently teaching ourselves to settle for spectacle, to be satisfied by titillation—and maybe even to become dependent on it—in our worship? Have we unintentionally allowed worship services to devolve into mere religious experiences? Have we mistaken the sizzle for the steak?

But imagine a different scenario. Imagine worship that has less to do with what we experience and more to do with God's experience of us. Imagine embracing a fuller definition of worship, one that begins in prayer closets and extends to soup kitchens. Imagine the power of the arts carried on the breath of the Holy Spirit. Imagine worship that is founded on a gospel that invites us to selflessness and humility and ultimately joy.

Transcendence in our worship is an encounter with the holy God in which we open the eyes of our hearts to his presence.

Spectacle can aid us in experiences of transcendence, but we must always be aware that in an increasingly self-absorbed culture, spectacle must always serve the still, small voice, and not the other way around.

MADE TO WORSHIP

There's a fascinating account in the book of Exodus, chapter 32. It speaks not only of the nature of celebrity but also of the very nature of humanity. It's the story of the quintessential idol: the golden calf.

We know the story. The nation Israel tires of waiting for Moses to come down from the mountain. They know their circumstances are the result of a series of miracles gifted to them by a gracious God. Yet they can't wait. They burn with the need to worship, so they create with their own hands a false idol, molded from the spoils of their oppressors, which they proceed to worship and glorify. Seeking transcendence, they settle for mere spectacle. On many levels, their actions are irrational, immoral, absurd. And yet there are parallels to worship today.

Moses, who carried the tablets containing the Ten Commandments, was so distraught at the sight of this false worship that he cast down the tablets at the foot of the mountain, breaking them. He burned the golden calf to a powder and made them drink it, internalizing their sin. And after some creative blame-shifting by Aaron ("Really, Moses, I just cast this gold in the fire, and this calf popped out!"), Moses had the perpetrators killed.

There is an obvious lesson here. We humans were made to worship something. It is hardwired into our souls. Lacking a clear understanding of God and having a natural predisposition toward ourselves, we make our own gods to venerate and worship. Psychologist Dr. Gerald May contends,

> From a psychoanalytic perspective, one could say we displace our longing for God upon other things; we cathect them instead of God. Behaviorally, we are conditioned to seek objects by the positive and negative reinforcements of our own private experience. . . . We look for ultimate satisfaction in God's palpable and definable creations instead of looking through them to the hidden, loving face of their Creator.[6]

We live in an increasingly spectacle-driven culture that inadvertently feeds our inborn need for transcendence and worship. This is why we uphold and revere our celebrities and athletes and pop stars and political leaders to such a high degree. Worship is foundational to who we are. Just go to an NFL game or rock concert or political rally—worship is happening, in fundamentally primal ways.

God knows this about us, of course, and he fashioned the first commandment to address it: "I am the LORD your God, who brought you out of Egypt, out of the land of slavery. You shall have no other gods before me" (Exodus 20:2-3). It's the first commandment, and it sets the tone for the rest of the commandments: that we are to put God and his will and ways first and foremost in our lives and hearts.

REFLECTIONS OF OUR CULTURE

Certainly, there are powerful and invisible forces tugging at the hearts of worshipers today. That being said, modern worship—in all its various flavors and forms—is simply a reflection of the culture around it. It reflects our culture's aesthetic and style, but more ominously, its values and motivations. Cultural values—like trendiness and superficiality and relativism—are deeply imbedded in these modern forms, whether we like it or not. And we must be aware of the attendant dangers. Culture is neither static nor amoral.

One of the deeply held misconceptions in churches is that the "product" (to use the term crassly) of church ministry is what happens on stage—the music and the programming and all the many elements of the service. But decades of full-time vocational ministry have taught me that great music, great art, and great programming are not the product—they are the byproduct. The true product of church ministry is the hearts of the people. Everything that comes from the stage—from the lighting design to the songs sung to the prayers prayed to the sermon preached—should be seen as a byproduct of submissive hearts that are growing in Christ.

We are indeed living in an exciting time in the life of the church. In the tempest of this high-tech information age, we have a tremendous opportunity to reach different generations in many different ways. And we must—with the best of our abilities, with the best of what we have, and with the best of who we are. Through it all, however, we must remain diligent against the darker, subterranean motivations that can seep into us—to be entertained, to seek emotional escape, to settle for experiences of God instead of God himself.

We must not mistake the smoke for the Spirit.

WORSHIP PRACTICE

Surprisingly, many people have very limited experiences in terms of worship style. We certainly like our comfort zones, even to the point of sitting in the same pew every week. But there is a wide variety of valid worship expressions—liturgical, charismatic, meditative, contemporary, traditional, modern. And we can get a bigger picture of our very big God when we learn to worship in the variety and scope of God's expressive people.

As a suggested practice, attend a church that is far different from the one you attend. If you have a large home church, attend a small one. If your church is loud and musical, attend a quiet, liturgical one. If you church is traditional with a choir and organ, attend one with a rock band. If you live in the suburbs, attend an inner-city church. The point is to get out of your comfort zone and your personal preferences. As you worship in this place, intend to fully seek God. See if he meets you there, and see if he has something to tell you.

Two

FIRST-PERSON SINGULAR

Your kingdom come,
your will be done,
on earth as it is in heaven.

MATTHEW 6:9-10

I HAD JUST COME OFF THE PLATFORM at a church service with the worship team, and judging by the responsiveness of the people, I thought that we had served our congregation fairly well. As I walked quietly to the back of the auditorium, I was stopped by someone attending the service.

Pulling me to his side, he quietly whispered, "Thanks for leading us this morning." I smiled in response. Then he added with great sincerity, "It was just the way I like it."

I think about that response often. It rattled me in that moment, and rattles me to this day. Obviously he offered that statement to me as a compliment. But it certainly didn't hit me that way.

CULTURAL NARCISSISM

"How many lead singers does it take to change a light bulb?" goes the well-worn joke. "One. She holds it in her hand, and the world revolves around her."

Narcissism has two general definitions: a clinical one and a social one. While they're related, it's important to distinguish between the two. Clinical narcissism is a personality disorder characterized by a person's overestimation of himself (abilities, looks, attributes, successes) and an excessive need for admiration and attention.[1] This narcissism is understood to be driven more from a hidden self-loathing rather than self-love. This person may be self-destructive and practice high-risk behaviors. Cultural narcissism is more subtle but vastly more pervasive. It can be described as a general self-centeredness and self-absorption, but at the societal level. It's accompanied by a great tolerance for people who are attention-grabbing, self-seeking, self-promoting, and self-gratifying, to the degree that such behaviors become the social norm.

Let's assume that a generation ago you knew someone who regularly took pictures of herself at different places, had them developed at the local twenty-four-hour photo, and then posted them on public bulletin boards around the neighborhood. What would you think about that person? Or let's assume that, a generation ago, you knew someone who would place ads in the classified section of the newspaper. But instead of selling something, these ads displayed photos of plates of food: barbecued salmon, pancakes, protein shakes, Big Macs. It may make some sense if he were a food critic, but many of the photos were of fast-food items or entrees he made himself. What would you think of him? What if a third person you knew, also a generation ago, called you a half dozen times a day? These short, random calls comprised a running commentary on her day—her thoughts, her activities, her political leanings, her emotions. You never asked her about her day; she simply felt it was important that you knew about it.

Perhaps you think these people are a little weird, and you even question their sanity. Certainly, a generation ago all of these behaviors would seem eccentric at best and certifiable at worst. But in this age of Facebook, Instagram, and Twitter, such conduct is commonplace, ordinary, almost obligatory.

Of course, not all individuals who take selfies or post pics of their dinners are narcissists. What I'm contending is that a generation ago, social mores and simple propriety would have leaned us toward a less self-focused expression. Such petty conceits would have been implicitly discouraged. But now the social filters that would keep us from such behaviors are lifted. Of course people want to see photos of me. Of course people are interested in what I had for dinner. Of course people need to hear my political opinions. It's the way we are now. It's simply the expression of our culture.

Prominent examples of our cultural narcissism surround us. Reality TV. Self-branding. Body sculpting. Paparazzi. Social media. Personal shoppers. Online gaming avatars. Cosmetic surgery. Fantasy sports. Prosperity theology. American exceptionalism. Generational entitlement.

If these were isolated, you might begin to suspect a degree of narcissism. But they're not isolated. And that's the point. In the span of a generation, narcissistic behaviors and attitudes have become not only normal but prevalent and even customary.

This cultural narcissism is propagated by celebrities, public figures, and other opinion leaders, who set the scale for what is acceptable behavior. Dr. Drew Pinsky contends that the narcissism of celebrities is becoming more and more normalized through the "celebrity-industrial complex" of social media, paparazzi, broadcast, and internet sites.[2] Early examples of this include entertainment news like TMZ and *People Magazine*, reality shows like *Keeping Up with the Kardashians* and *The Osbournes*, red-carpet events, and the ever-present media. When someone has a wardrobe incident, a feud with a fellow star, a stint in rehab, or an appearance at a new hot nightclub, we seem to know about it.

Consider the seven traits classically associated with clinical narcissism listed by Pinsky: "authority, entitlement, exhibitionism, exploitativeness, self-sufficiency, superiority, and vanity."[3] We see all these traits exhibited publicly more and more by performers, politicians, sports figures, and others that traditionally become our role models. And then we see them reflected by the society at large. Thus, individuals at all levels are trending toward an increasing narcissism, thinking of themselves first before others in ways that have become normalized in society. Jean Twenge and Keith Campbell assert in their book *The Narcissism Epidemic*, "Not only are there more narcissists than ever, but non-narcissistic people are seduced by the increasing emphasis on material wealth, physical appearance, celebrity worship, and attention seeking. Standards have shifted, sucking otherwise humble people into the vortex."[4]

Society has changed. We are led to believe that our children must succeed in school and sports, not primarily for themselves but to make us look like better parents. Our spouses are trophies, or they're discarded for new trophies. Our possessions are seen as reflections of who we are, not necessities for living. Our careers have become measurements of our status, so many ladders to be climbed. Our paychecks are mere instruments of our vanities, not opportunities for generosity. But this is not the way of Jesus.

The life of the Christ-follower is marked by an increasing love for God and people, and a decreasing love of the things of the world. We deny ourselves, take up his cross, and follow him (Mark 8:34). On this path, we learn to live an other-centric life, without selfishness or ego or vice, as we learn more and more to be like Jesus. We're encouraged "to put off your old self, which is being corrupted by its deceitful desires; to be made new in the attitude of your minds; and to put on the new self, created to be like God in true righteousness and holiness" (Ephesians 4:22-25).

Cultural narcissism is in direct conflict with the gospel, for it's the very opposite of dying to oneself. Narcissism is the self in excess, a grandiose view of one's talents, appearance, needs, and life that seeks attention and importance. Narcissism is contrary to a life of discipleship and spiritual formation. And it's contrary to the communal, ecclesiastical nature of our faith, which calls us to love and serve one another. In small and large degree, it works in opposition to a gospel that invites us to another way.

NARCISSISM IN OUR WORSHIP

A number of years ago, I did an unscientific but exhaustive poll. I asked everyone around me, perhaps a hundred people, the simple question "What is your definition of *good* worship? How do you know the worship was *good*?" I found that there's an unspoken but widely held notion that worship can be measured by how you feel during the worship time. Usually people say something like "I was really moved by the worship." Or "I really felt

God this morning." Or "I felt like I forgot all of my problems." Or "I really liked the music."

All of these answers may have some validity and appropriateness. And all of them seem sincere and heartfelt. But imbedded in them is an insidious recurring theme: the word *I*. Narcissism has infiltrated even the way we worship God. We now measure how good the worship is based on how good it makes us feel.

But worship isn't about me as the center. Worship is about God. So perhaps a truer measure of worship isn't how we feel but how we make God feel. God is at the center of our worship. Maybe the answer to what makes "good" worship requires the question, "Was God pleased by our worship?" And we know what pleases God: a humble and pure heart, giving worship without agenda or reservation. The psalmist declared,

> Who may ascend the mountain of the LORD?
> Who may stand in his holy place?
> The one who has clean hands and a pure heart,
> who does not trust in an idol
> or swear by a false god.

> They will receive blessing from the LORD
> and vindication from God their Savior. (Psalm 24:3-5)

At one point in my life, I felt called to help lead a large church that was experiencing a worship war. Two camps—one traditional and the other contemporary—were in conflict over stylistic preferences. A church split was in the balance. Emotions were high and opinions were zealous. Because I was the new worship pastor, people were looking to see on which side of the fence I stood. I truly felt that both sides were, to varying degrees, missing the point of worship, which is primarily to love God and one another. So I helped convince the senior pastor to bring the traditional and contemporary services together, so we could begin the process of healing and fostering hearts of worship.

As you can imagine, every Sunday I felt like there was a target painted on my back. But time and loving perseverance eventually got us to the place where both sides were cordial, which made me hopeful for them. After one service, some older folks approached me to thank me for being true to the hymns I was leading. I expressed my appreciation for their support, but then added, "You know, I'm not playing the hymns for you. I'm playing the hymns because the younger generations need to learn how to worship God with them." With that, they wholeheartedly agreed. But before their smiles disappeared, I added kindly, "And the reason I'm playing the modern worship songs is so you can learn how to worship God with them too."

Because a narcissistic worldview has become so imbedded in us, we have inadvertently created unspoken criteria for worship, and then appointed ourselves the judges of it. But this is not the way of the kingdom. So the next time you want to rate the worship on a Sunday morning, I encourage you not to look at the band or the song selection or the style or quality of music. Look into *yourself.* Ask, "Did I come with a pure and humble heart? Did I give my worship freely to God? Did I come prepared and motivated to worship? Did I put aside my own tendencies to be a consumer of worship? Did I love God today?"

These other-centric questions may be a truer measure of whether the worship was good or not. How we feel is not the product of worship. How we feel is a byproduct of worship.

WORSHIPING IN THE PRONOUNS

At a national worship conference, I had the opportunity to be led in worship with the most recently released worship songs. Each song was played and led with great skill, and they were well written and emotionally engaging. They rocked hard and sounded great. But something in the back of my mind began to gnaw at me as one new song after another was unveiled.

I struggled with this gnawing the entire first day of the conference. And then it hit me. All the songs played that day were subjective, not objective. In other words, the lyrics were dependent on the personal experiences or perceptions of the lyricist, not based on the objective truths of the Bible. That isn't a bad thing by itself. But in light of our increasingly narcissistic society, this subjectivity can inadvertently feed a self-centered faith.

Once again, risking the alienation of my readers, let me give you a few examples. Consider the line "You are worthy of my praise," which has shown up in a variety of songs. Now carefully reconsider that lyric. The Bible often refers to God in this way: "The Lord, who is worthy of praise," which defines God rightly as the center of our worship.[5] But in my searching, I couldn't find any Scripture that states "worthy of *my* praise." Hidden in that lyric is an unspoken egocentricity—almost an audacity—that places us at the center of the worship experience instead of God. It implies "I have experienced God, and I have found him worthy." While I believe the narcissism is unintended, it's implied just the same.

Consider another lyrical phrase: "You died to set me free." Is this a true statement? Yes. It's certainly true that Jesus lived, died, and rose again for our sake. But to say that Jesus died to set *me* free implies an unintended self-centeredness. When we sing this type of lyric in a congregational setting, it ignores the saving grace given to all those singing around us and makes us focus on our own grace alone. This can be true for all songs that lean heavily on an "I" emphasis in the lyrics; worship can be reduced to the relationship between the single worshiper and God, ignoring the very essence of worship in community.

There is profound truth in this lyric. But the truth can be lost in the malaise of our cultural narcissism, as we inadvertently place the emphasis on the single worshiper, not on he who is worshiped. Related to this second example is the lyric form that states, in effect, "You [did this in my life], and that's why I worship." Though the implied meaning is unintended, this lyrical form not only makes it me-centered but also makes our worship conditional to God's ability to meet our needs.

Consider this last example: "God, I want more of you." It's very true that our love for God creates a greater yearning for him. But in light of the cultural narcissism we live in, this lyric can express a desire for experiences of God instead of worship of God. This lyrical form can be a profound statement of our deepest need, or it can deteriorate into a demanding statement of our most selfish neediness. Once again, this isn't intended by the songwriter. But like a child whining for ice cream, Christians influenced by cultural narcissism can turn this honest yearning into an egocentric demand.

Perhaps the common practice of using a continuous selection of "I" and "me" songs reveals how cultural narcissism has seeped into our worship. At this particular worship conference, almost every one of the songs I heard was first-person singular (I, me, mine). Given the context of much of modern worship—darkened sanctuaries where the visual focus isn't on the community worshiping together but on each individual's expression of worship—one can see how this can feed the cultural narcissism in us.

This is in marked contrast to the worship described in the book of Revelation, the worship of the Lamb, where all the songs are ascriptive—that is, they ascribe glory to God. Lyrics, prayers, and exaltations are addressed to God in the second-person singular (for example, *you, your, thine*). There is never a *me* or *my* or *I* in Revelation worship. As Rory Noland remarked, "Worship that is pure ascription—focused not on us, but solely on God—gets our eyes off ourselves and onto the Lord. It is a biblical way to worship!"[6]

Please understand that I'm not critical of these songs when they're used in a proper worship context. I believe that fully formed worship should reflect an appropriate use of all the pronouns—*we* (the people gathered), *you* (trinitarian expressions of Father, Son, and Spirit), *he* (declarations of God's nature and deeds), and *I* (personal responses). All of these words contribute to the vertical and horizontal dialogue that makes up congregational worship. But a constant diet of subjective lyrical forms can unintentionally define God according to our experience of God, instead of defining God according to his biblical and manifest revelation. When we make experience a necessary condition of truth, we unintendedly adopt a postmodern worldview and attach it to our faith. For centuries, personal theologies have been formed as much by the lyrics we sing as by the Bible we read. Words matter, because words convey ideas. And a steady diet of subjective lyrics unintentionally feeds the cultural narcissism that already knocks at the doors of our congregations.

Cultural narcissism can seep into many other aspects of our worship as well. Prayer, public and private, can be reduced to petitionary lists, asking God to do things for us. Our spiritual vocabulary often seems to lack the other important aspects of prayer, including adoration, confession, and thanksgiving. This may be why ancient prayers, creeds, and psalms, which help to fortify our prayer language, are now being incorporated into worship by more congregations.

Cultural narcissism also affects our sermons. From the sermon illustrations we employ to the feel-good subjects of our messages, we're all in danger of allowing a narcissistic worldview to skew how we present the truth and how that truth is perceived by our culturally influenced congregations. Further, church branding is inherently fraught with narcissistic dangers. Branding is, in a sense, a form of image management, and advertising is, in a sense, a form of bragging.

Finally, our cultural self-centeredness is betrayed by our chronological context. We treat worship as having a beginning and an end. Some churches even incorporate a countdown screen to indicate that the event is about to begin. But in the big picture, worship is not an event. It's an ongoing act that occurs eternally throughout creation. Worship takes place in heaven and on earth (dimension); in the past, present, and future (time); and all around the world (place).

I recently got a chance to walk along the beach in Santa Cruz, California. It's a wonderful feeling: the sand between your toes, the surf ebbing and flowing at your ankles, the swooshing sound of the water. At one point I stopped to watch the water move around my legs, to watch my feet sink slowly into the sand. And then I thought about how vast the ocean is, how wide and deep and long, how powerful and unknowable.

Worshiping God is like that too. When our churches gather on a Sunday morning, we merely step into the vastness of worship, like dipping our feet into the surf of an immense and ever-dynamic ocean of praise. When we worship, we join the church down the street, house churches in China, Christians dancing in Uganda, Christians rocking out in Australia, persecuted Christians in India and the Middle East, prison chapels and convalescent home fellowships. And we enter into the worship of the angels in the heavenlies, who sing the eternal song, along with all of creation throughout the entire universe. When we worship on a Sunday morning, we should be aware of the greater significance of what it is we join. It is not about us in more ways than we are even aware.

SEEING CLEARLY

Image magnification, or IMAG, is the projection of images of people on stage onto the screens that are also used for lyrics and sermon notes. IMAG is used primarily in large venues, where on-stage personalities are too small to see with the naked eye, and therefore video magnification is used to augment the communication of the message. I continue to be surprised by the number of moderate-sized churches that use IMAG. I have been to several medium-sized churches in which the IMAG image of the preaching pastor was about the same size as the pastor in real life.

As worshipers, we have become so conditioned by our cultural narcissism that we no longer see it. In the case of the medium-sized church, the true and legitimate reason for IMAG was lost to the idea that they wanted to adopt megachurch practices.

We began this chapter by teasing the Facebookers, Instagramers, and Tweeters. We end with a sober warning that our society will continue to become more vain, more self-centered, more outrageous, and more oblivious. To what degree is this harming our souls? And how do we as followers of Jesus respond? I believe it begins by attuning ourselves to the cultural narcissism that's around us, both in its nuanced subtlety and in its blatant vulgarity. Only then can we respond to it, both individually and as church bodies, leaning into God for discernment and correction.

The gospel invitation given by Jesus includes learning to live an other-centric life:

> Whoever wants to be my disciple must deny themselves and take up their cross and follow me. For whoever wants to save their life will lose it, but whoever loses their life for me and for the gospel will save it. What good is it for someone to gain the whole world, yet forfeit their soul? Or what can anyone give in exchange for their soul? (Mark 8:34-37)

Jesus is saying that following him includes dying to oneself and one's agenda and self-orientation. And then he says something even more startling: you can find true fulfillment only by surrendering your life to him. Following Christ is not so much about seeking self-fulfillment as it is about willing self-denial. It means being consumed by God and living for his glory. In the process of loving God and loving others, we find ourselves not at the center, but joyfully at the periphery of the throne. Worship can and should be this way.

James K. A. Smith argues in his book *You Are What You Love* that there are competing and rival liturgies everywhere. So there's a liturgy to a baseball game, a liturgy to a movie theater, even a liturgy to the shopping mall. And these liturgies—these formularies—shape us in good and bad ways. His point: "We become what we worship because we worship what we love."[7] Our hearts are molded by the things we love and shaped by the prescriptions of these loves. A lifetime of living in our cultural narcissism has trained us to love material things, follow our unmet desires, and chase what will never satisfy us. The liturgies of cultural narcissism have trained us too well.

Perhaps Augustine puts this in a more hopeful light. In his *Confessions*, he earnestly writes, "You have made us for Yourself, and our heart is restless until it rests in You."[8] God does not want us to be unhappy and discomforted in our worship. Quite the contrary. He desires to meet our truest desires, desires that are much deeper and more mysterious than we can describe. But this requires surrender—of our own petty preferences, our comfort zones, our wills. Ultimately we must rid ourselves of the need to meet God on our terms.

In those times of surrender we might find God waiting for us, ready to fulfill our deepest need.

WORSHIP PRACTICE

The word *narcissist* comes from the ancient Greek myth of Narcissus, a young man who fell in love with his reflection in water. While this sounds ludicrous, it points out how culturally universal narcissism and self-centeredness is. Narcissism is an expression of the self, and a good practice to combat our selfishness is to focus on others.

Find a place where you can serve in an other-centric way. Offer to serve at your local food bank, soup kitchen, homeless shelter, preschool, or convalescent home. Do this individually or with a friend or even a small group. When we focus on the needs of others instead of ourselves, our view of the world—and of ourselves—becomes more appropriately proportioned. And ironically we receive a satisfaction that's deeper than the superficial satisfactions we derive from our selfishness.

Three

FALLING ON MY FACE

The very credentials these people are waving around
as something special, I'm tearing up and throwing
out with the trash—along with everything else I used
to take credit for. And why? Because of Christ. Yes,
all the things I once thought were so important are
gone from my life. Compared to the high privilege of
knowing Christ Jesus as my Master, firsthand, everything
I once thought I had going for me is insignificant—
dog dung. I've dumped it all in the trash so that I
could embrace Christ and be embraced by him.

PHILIPPIANS 3:7-8 *THE MESSAGE*

LONG AGO, I KNEW A YOUNG MAN. Competent, talented, creative, driven, he was a worship leader at the church I attended. As is often the case in start-up churches, the most talented musician in the room is assigned the role of worship leader, regardless of calling or skill set or theological training. Our church had just adopted a seeker-style strategy of ministry, and it had finally become feasible to offer a full-time position in the worship arts. Armed with equal parts bravery and naiveté, he accepted the position and immersed himself fully in the cause.

This likeable young man had a high motor and equally high ambitions, so it wasn't long before he began to attract other talented musicians. Rock, pop, jazz, country, and other styles became regular flavors on the menu. Adopting a popular, high-tech style of ministry, theatrical lighting, multimedia, and a high-decibel sound system soon followed. Theater-quality drama, sometimes poignant and sometimes outrageous, became a regular feature in our services. So did fast-paced video and other artistic elements. In some carefully crafted branding, our church adopted the tagline "You'll be surprised." And our services delivered.

Soon there was a buzz about our church—not just in the pews but also out in the coffee houses, at kids' soccer games, in the aisles of the local supermarkets. Something was happening at the church, and people all over the community wanted to be a part of it. Attendance climbed quickly, and services were added. In just a few years our church was running five services per week, with Sunday mornings having standing room only.

The idea of a renegade church preaching an easy-to-understand gospel appealed to many, and a good many people were making decisions to follow Jesus during this time. With strong pastoral leadership and a compelling vision, the church began to see marked growth. For this, our congregation was both grateful and impassioned. More attenders meant more giving, which meant a bigger budget. Staff was added to serve the needs of the ever-growing congregation, and our church necessarily moved to a more formal corporate structure of leadership. We purchased land and began making big plans for the future.

The worship leader's ambitions grew with the church. There were now five staff people just in the worship arts ministries, which was more than the entire staff when he had started. His team began to record albums, publish their original drama sketches, and put on large-scale concerts. The pastors and performers of our church became local celebrities. We even had our own merchandising, from T-shirts to coffee mugs to license plate frames. Soon we were caught up in a multimillion-dollar building campaign, raising support for a three-phase church campus with the final goal of a 2,400-seat auditorium. It seemed everyone was caught up in the adrenaline rush.

The young man maintained some semblance of a quiet demeanor through it all. He loved the Lord and genuinely felt it a privilege to be a part of God's work in the world. But behind the noble intentions, he loved the rush of success, loved the accolades, loved sitting in the buzz of it all, and most of all, loved placing his identity in being the worship arts pastor of a fast-growing, upscale church. In the darkest parts of himself, it had become his drug, and he was addicted to it.

Eventually, inevitably, cracks began to form in the soul of the young man. He was a good guy, moral, earnest, levelheaded, and God-fearing. He wouldn't have been hired if he hadn't been. But he was a musician, an artist, a human being. And that often means a strange concoction of fears and doubts, insecurities and anxieties, goals and aspirations, secret dreams and hidden angst. Artists are generally a little off-center. After all, they're creatives with complex temperaments and unique ways of expressing themselves. If there are tattoos in the sanctuary, chances are the worship leader is the one wearing them.

Pastors, ministers, and worship leaders feel unique pressures to perform, to be authentic and whole (especially on stage), to always be the most talented person in the building. They're on trial every week—compared, applauded, and critiqued. There are also pressures to build teams, administrate programs, incorporate the latest technologies, and create splashy events. On top of it all are the pressures to be perfect parents, perfect spouses, perfect friends. While these pressures might be unique to church leaders, at some level I believe all people experience them in their own ways.

In the deep recesses of this young man's soul was a need for acceptance and approval, which he fed with a performance addiction and anesthetized with ego-feeding activities. So he often worked sixty-hour weeks. He also performed in a popular band outside the church. He took on added projects. More often than he would admit, he allowed the busyness of church to replace time with God.

This is one of the ironies of ministry: the things of God often keep us from God himself. Unfortunately, many fast-growing churches are unprepared for the soul-sapping nature of ministry. In fact, churches may inadvertently encourage the fast pace and workaholism that come with ministry success. But that success has a cost.

At the center of this young man's blind spot was pride. Success as well as failure can expose one's humanity. He began to quarrel privately with the leadership, insisting on more creative control. He had been performing his own original worship songs and dramas in church, but he started arguing over copyright issues. He also began battling his internal demons: fear of failure, approval issues, insecurity. Although he tried to be honest with his feelings of pride and hold himself accountable to others, it was natural for him to hide behind a false self, which even he didn't fully comprehend. And frankly, he liked the applause and fame more than he could admit.

Eventually the situation became untenable, both for him and for the church leadership. At the height of their shared "success," they agreed to part ways.

THE TRUTH ABOUT OURSELVES

Well, if you haven't figured this out yet, the young man in the story is me.[1] I was that ambitious, workaholic, approval-driven worship pastor. I was the one who, in an effort to further the kingdom, ended up building his own little one in the process. I was the one who had to come face to face with my ego, my dysfunctions, my pride. And in the process, I had to come face to face with God himself.

The role of a worship leader is to lead people to the throne of God, but we can often make it about ourselves in ways we don't even understand. Because of my internal wiring and my family-of-origin issues, it was natural for me to attach my identity to what I did more than to who I served.

The truth is, we are all masters of self-deception. To varying degrees, we're all unaware of our own complex and multilayered junk. This is equally true for the worship leader on stage and the worshiper in the pew. That junk keeps us from worshiping God in the fullness that he intended. The shame, fear, neediness, and dysfunctions that mar our souls are the distorted lenses that keep us from seeing God clearly, from loving him purely, from worshiping him more fully.

If you relate to my story in any way, then I appreciate your transparency and self-awareness. If you don't, you just might be in denial. Every single one of us—without exception—carries with us the foibles of our humanity. And this affects how we are able to give God our honest worship.

Many of us have this mistaken notion that we can somehow impress God. So we volunteer to work in high-visibility ministries, go on impressive mission trips, and insist on always being prettied-up, holier versions of ourselves on Sunday morning. We're drawn to churches that appear successful and to church leaders who reflect that success. Or, in the secular arenas, we work our way up corporate ladders, drive new cars, live in big houses, and fight and claw for the American dream, all the while trying to give everyone the impression that we are purpose-driven and our kids are grown God's way. But the truth is that we can't impress God, can't pretend before him, can't hide our true selves from him.

At the end of days, God won't say to us, "Well done, good and *successful* servant." Nor will he will say, "Well done, good and *religious* servant." He will say, "Well done, good and faithful servant!" (Matthew 25:21, 23). Ultimately, God won't reward us according to the numbers we so often use as metrics for ministry success or according to our ability to be doctrinally correct and religiously devout. He will reward us for our faithfulness to the calling he gave us. For continuing to follow our calling regardless of the circumstances. For continuing to love those he has called us to love, regardless of their lovability. For responding in increasing faith to God's faithfulness to us. Fidelity—being faithful to a person, cause, or belief, demonstrated by continuing loyalty and support—may be a truer metric of success in God's economy. It's in the living out of fidelity, integrity, and congruence that real depth of meaning is found in ministry, in marriage, in family, in a local church, and in all of life.

I eventually began to understand that growing my soul as a worshiper meant I needed to confront the pride that was marbled deep in my flesh. And we all have pride issues—it is ingrained in our humanity. Thankfully, God's gracious invitation to us is to take the journey from self-destructive pride to life-giving humility. And he patiently walks this journey with us.

PRIDE OF PLACE

Pride is the universal sin of exalting ourselves and placing our own interests above the interests of others, and especially of God. C. S. Lewis stated that pride "is the complete anti-God state of mind."[2] Saint Augustine said, "It was Pride that changed angels into devils; it is humility that makes men as angels." And the book of Proverbs warns us that "Pride goes before destruction, a haughty spirit before a fall" (Proverbs 16:18). Pride is not only one of the seven deadly sins (including envy, gluttony, lust, anger, greed, and sloth); theologians and philosophers consider it the gateway from which all other sins emanate. In other words, the initial sin that births all other sins is to choose our own way before and above God's way, to be self-seeking.

Pride takes on many forms. It can be overt like a rap song or sublime like a passing response of one who has false humility. Pride can take the form of excessive egotism or, in the opposite extreme, deeply held insecurities that manifest in obsessive control or perfectionism. Pride is tied to self-worth, self-loathing, self-absorption, self-centeredness. But pride is also the only one of the deadly sins that is culturally acceptable. We have pride in our country, pride in our work, pride in our sports teams. Pride implies an element of self-respect and self-esteem, something we teach, model, and value. Thus, the sin of pride can be easy to disguise and justify.

This is why pride is so opposed to worship. Pride feeds itself with admiration and recognition, with being in the spotlight, with the attention of others. But the intent of worship is to glorify the one true God in our actions, our words, our thoughts, and our intentions. In worship, we not only lay down our struggles, fears, and sins, we also lay down our need for attention and self-centeredness. For worship is not about us. Worship is other-centered and upward-focused by nature. It's all about our holy, holy, holy God. At least that's the way it should be.

A. W. Tozer tells a story that goes like this: Jesus fulfilled Scripture when he rode a young donkey into Jerusalem (described in John 12:12-16). The great crowds came to meet him, taking palm branches and spreading them out before him, praising his name, shouting, "Hosanna! Hosanna!" The donkey, looking around at the crowd, thought, *Wow! I must really be great!*[3]

In the grand scheme of things, pastors and church leaders like me have to remember that we're just the donkey. Our role is that of servant worshipers. And all of us are to carry Jesus to his rightful place, to lift him up, and to help those we lead and those worshiping with us to come before him so that they lift him up as well.

The life and words of the apostle Paul have been a great encouragement to me in my own journey. Born to an elite family, afforded the rights of Roman citizenry, a credentialed scholar, a famed zealot of the law, Paul took a faith journey from the heights of pride to the valleys of humility through the rivers of grace. Originally known as Saul, he was a tenacious and single-minded persecutor who struck fear among the first-century followers of the Way. By his own estimation, he was to the right of righteousness, "faultless" (Philippians 3:4-8). And then one day, while hunting Christians, he was struck by a blinding light on the road to Damascus. He had an encounter with the living God. And he was never the same. Fully captured by the grace of God, Paul faithfully preached the gospel of Jesus Christ in spite of shipwrecks and imprisonments and numerous beatings and tortures, even to his death. Paul's encounter put into perspective who God truly was and who Paul was before God. He would later write of his boasting: "Compared to the high privilege of knowing Christ Jesus as my Master, firsthand, everything I once thought I had going for me is insignificant—dog dung. I've dumped it all in the trash so that I could embrace Christ and be embraced by him" (Philippians 3:8-9 *The Message*).

Paul's story and mine have some common themes: A wrong understanding of one's place before God. A need to place one's worth in one's own accomplishments. Confusing religiosity with relationship. I take great solace in knowing that God redeemed Paul and called him to a greatness that comes only through humility. Far beyond the first century, his example and influence still encourage and edify us today.

IT'S NOT THE HEAT, IT'S THE HUMILITY

The antithesis of pride is humility. And it's also the antidote. Humility is a pathway toward increased intimacy with and love for God. So for the worshiper, one of our greatest ambitions should be humility.

Here's a working definition: humility is *truly knowing who you are before God*. Paul reminds us in his letter to the Romans, "Do not think of yourself more highly than you ought, but rather think of yourself with sober judgment, in accordance with the faith God has distributed to each of you" (Romans 12:3). What Paul calls for is not false humility, the feigned act of modesty. Nor is it self-deprecation, being critical of oneself to the point of disparagement. Humility is having a proper and personal understanding of who God is and then understanding who we truly are in light of that awareness.

This definition has far-reaching implications regarding how we take our place in the body of Christ, how we live out our faith to the world, and especially how we worship. If worship is, at its core, how we love our good and gracious God through the actions and intentions of our lives, then humility—truly knowing who we are before God—is at the foundation of our relationship. So I encourage you to hold on to this definition of humility and take it into the next few chapters.

Jesus is of course the model of what humility is and how we can live it. Paul eloquently describes this in his counsel to the Philippians:

> Do nothing out of selfish ambition or vain conceit. Rather, in humility value others above yourselves, not looking to your own interests but each of you to the interests of the others.
>
> In your relationships with one another, have the same mindset as Christ Jesus:
>
> Who, being in very nature God,
>
> did not consider equality with God something to be

> used to his own advantage;
> rather, he made himself nothing
>> by taking the very nature of a servant,
>> being made in human likeness.
> And being found in appearance as a man,
>> he humbled himself
>> by becoming obedient to death—
>>> even death on a cross! (Philippians 2:3-8)

According to this definition, humility is a death of sorts. It is dying to ourselves, our own interests, our own ways, our own false identities, our own need to control. And then it is surrendering to God, rightfully allowing him to give our lives direction and purpose and worth. Humility is the truth of who you are in light of who God is. And this is the best part: in God's eyes, we are not who we pretend to be—we are infinitely more than that. To know who we truly are before God is the easy yoke and light burden that Jesus invites us to wear.

A "PERSONAL" GOD

Evangelicals often refer to our relationship with Jesus as a "personal" one. And while this is very true, it is often misapplied. The word *personal* does not mean "individual" or "private," like having your own personal shopper at Nordstrom. It means intimate. It means deeply relational. It means intensely communal. So while our relationship with Jesus is personal, it is not intended to be private. Christianity is a communal faith. It is a "one another" type of faith. Jesus is the groom, and together we are the bride of Christ, the church.

Unfortunately, we often take this misunderstood idea of personal relationship and attach it to our worship experience. Thus worship is understood not primarily as a communal action between God and his people, but as a group of individual experiences happening simultaneously in the same room. There's a rampant individualism happening in our worship sanctuaries, fueled by our cultural narcissism and masked by our need for spectacle. And this individualism feeds our egocentrism, our pride. But worship is primarily outside of us, not internalized in us—worship begins and ends not in our hearts but in the heart of God.

One of the essential principles of worship is that we don't worship solely as individuals, but rather we experience worship most fully when we enter in through community. We are a people united by our common faith in Jesus; we have been made into one entity called the church. The church is not a group of individuals each finding God on their own, nor is worship a group of individuals each communing with God on their own. The church in its very essence and nature is a community, and worship is more fully formed in community. We are like strings in a long ornate tapestry, each contributing a thread in a beautiful picture that God weaves in the universe. Outside of the tapestry the string loses meaning. Thus, as we are gathered, we are more ourselves than when we are apart.

Humility is the language that allows us to mutually submit to one another in community. When we truly understand who we are before a loving God—marred by sin, loved by God, saved by grace—then together we have the marvelous opportunity to truly be the church as it is intended. Christianity is, at its best, a life-shared faith.

FACING UP

Until recent history, those who led musical worship were positioned either in the loft at the back of the sanctuary or far off to the side of the main stage. While they could be heard, singers and instrumentalists weren't the visual center point of the worship. This was not only because of aesthetics and acoustics; leaders understood that worship, like liturgy, is the work of the people. They understood that the proper posture of worship is, symbolically, with one's face to the ground.

Søren Kierkegaard is said to have likened the worship service to the theater.[4] He posited that most people believe that the pastors and worship leaders are the performers, God is the director, and the congregation is the audience. But this is an incorrect paradigm. In truth, the pastors and worship leaders are the directors, the congregation are the performers, and God is rightfully the audience.

While worship bands and choirs may no longer be heard and not seen, we should still take a cue from our worship forebears in a spiritual sense. The role and calling of the worship leader is to be a servant; we are to serve our congregations with our voices, our talents, and our lives. We are carriers of the presence of God for our communities of faith (Deuteronomy 10:8).[5] And the role of the worshiper is to take ourselves out of the center of worship and put God in that place, fully focused on our audience of One.

In the Bible, falling on one's face was a normal and understandable response to encountering God (Ezekiel 43:1-5). For me, falling on my face has an obvious double meaning. It means to fail spectacularly. And it also means to assume an extreme posture of humility before God. I know that I have failed many times, both publicly before others and privately in the inner workings of my own heart. But it is in these failings that God offers his gracious hand to pull us from the turbulent tide of our own self-centeredness and into the calm waters of his will. Through both of these very real sets of personal experiences, I have found God to be the light unto my path and the lifter of my head (Psalms 119:105; 3:3).

Ultimately, I think the key is learning to see ourselves the way God sees us. For in our depravity we may not be as bad as we think. And though our salvation is secure, we may still have much to be saved from.

So what is the truth about ourselves? And what is honest worship? In asking these questions I believe we can reclaim the soul of the worshiper.

WORSHIP PRACTICE

One practical spiritual practice that helps us to renew our minds (Romans 12:2) is memorizing Scripture. This practice locks the words of Scripture into our brains so that we can recall them when needed. In light of this chapter, memorize Philippians 2:5-11, which shares powerful truths about who Jesus is and how he acted on our behalf, in step with the will of the Father. He is the model of humility.

Four

THE NATURE OF IDENTITY

The only accurate way to understand ourselves is
by what God is and by what he does for us, not
by what we are and what we do for him.

ROMANS 12:3 *THE MESSAGE*

MUCH IS SAID THESE DAYS about being authentic. We want authentic worship, authentic leadership, authentic community. But the reality is that authenticity is scary and daunting, a difficult virtue to live out. We are all walking wounded—carrying the baggage of our dysfunctional backgrounds, the consequences of our sins, the lies we've chosen to believe about ourselves. None of us is whole.

At the root of this thing I'm calling honest worship is the issue of identity. So it's necessary to unpack that a bit. As we do, know that what I share comes from my personal experience as a pastor, leader of artists, and fellow traveler on the spiritual journey. Again, I'm not a professional in the field of psychology.

A dozen years or so into my ministry career, I began to realize that my perception of myself wasn't how people experienced me. Some of the ways I acted and reacted were driven by emotional mechanisms deeply programmed into me. I had too much pride wrapped up in being a talented musician, a well-liked pastor, a leader of successful things. I had been meeting with my senior pastor about some of these issues—the kinds of issues that most churches just live with, but over time take their toll on relationships and ministries. He suggested that I work through these issues with a professional. In a sense, I was walking into the thicket of my soul, intent on pulling weeds.

Counseling wasn't easy for me.[1] It required me to lay down my agendas and self-perceptions. I also had to entertain the notion that I wasn't who I thought I was or who God intended me to be. It's not easy dismantling a lifetime of defense mechanisms, wrong perceptions, and self-perpetuated lies. After some weeks, the counselor explained to me that he saw me as a person who was fearful of criticism, and I had created complex interpersonal and emotional systems to help me avoid the truth about myself. "Criticism management" was the term he used. In that moment, he both shed light into some dark parts of my soul and caused a crisis of identity. I had to figure out who I really was.

Over time, I began to recognize that criticism management had roots in my childhood. I have two older half-brothers from my mother's first marriage who came to live with us when I was four years old. Throughout my childhood and adolescence, they were both my heroes and my bullies. As a child, my relationship with them was a complex web of trying to win their approval, avoiding conflict with them, and reacting to them in passive-aggressive ways.

My criticism management had become more amplified in my ministry, and it was a source of conflict and exasperation to the church staff. But the *why* was the real revelation.

At some point, we added a gifted teaching pastor to our church staff, and he soon formed a close partnership with our senior pastor. Which is a good thing. But I began subconsciously reacting negatively to this newly formed leadership duo, in the same way I had reacted to my two older brothers: I rebelled against their leadership in subtle and subversive ways. I argued with them, citing artistic control and conflict of vision. I silently resented their close friendship. I didn't understand that my highly tuned criticism management mechanisms that were formed in childhood were kicking in. I was reacting to my pastors—and I didn't even realize it. It took professional Christian counseling and the Spirit of God bringing me to the point of humility for me to see it.

As Christians, we believe that our faith journey includes deep personal change, which is often referred to as sanctification or spiritual formation. But I believe that there is some confusion as to the actual process. On one extreme, some believe that transformation is simply something that is done to us without any effort of our own (like magic), while at the other extreme, others believe it requires behavioral changes that we undertake (such as attending church, reading the Bible, and especially avoiding things like sinning, smoking, and swearing).

The truth is that we have all been spiritually formed (or deformed) by our past experiences, relationships, and internal programming. Spiritual transformation is what we are called to—in cooperation with the Holy Spirit and under the lordship of Jesus Christ—to re-form who we are from our past spiritual deformations. It is the invitation extended to the Romans, to "not conform to the pattern of this world, but be transformed by the renewing of your mind" (Romans 12:2). And it requires both the work of God in us and diligent effort and cooperation from us.

Spiritual transformation is much more than learning the Bible and trying to apply it to your life. It's surrendering to God the totality of both your conscious will and the psychological mechanisms that affect your will, including your addictions, wrong thinking, and false self. Walking in step with God isn't just trying to live a life of righteousness; it's also becoming a person for whom righteousness is natural and easy. So spiritual transformation is learning in greater and greater ways to embody the identity of our true self in Christ.

Through this journey, I began to understand that such psychological mechanisms were part of my false self, and they were keeping me from being the person God intended me to be—and by extension, the worshiper God intended me to be. God was calling me to live deeply in my true self and not in the false self I had built to keep him and others out.

THE FALSE SELF

We live in a fallen world, one that shapes us in ways we don't understand. Every family has dysfunctions, every person has blind spots, every shape has a shadow. The term *false self* refers to an identity we unconsciously form throughout our lives that disguises, undergirds, and protects us. It's false because it's based on an inner dialogue of self-sustaining lies, defense mechanisms, and conscious and subconscious pretending.[2]

Thomas Keating, a Roman Catholic monk and priest, wrote in his book *Invitation to Love*,

The particular consequences of original sin include all the self-serving habits that have been woven into our personalities from the time we were conceived; all the harm that other people have done to us knowingly and unknowingly at an age when we could not defend ourselves; and the methods we acquired, many of them now unconscious, to ward off the pain of unbearable situations. This constellation of pre-rational reactions is the foundation of the false self. The false self develops in opposition to the true self. Its center of gravity is the self as separate from God and others, and hence turned in on itself.[3]

The true self becomes encased by a callused shell of behaviors and wrong thinking to keep us happy and safe and to meet our need for fulfillment apart from God. None of us wants to feel naked and ashamed.[4] This is an issue of pride, in the broadest sense, for it speaks to our very identities: our false identity in the world and our true identity in Christ. God wishes to wean us from our false self and the power it has over us, so we can be genuine before God and other people, and truly live and worship in the truth.

The seventh chapter of the book of Romans poses a very confusing but very human dilemma. It states,

> I know that good itself does not dwell in me, that is, in my sinful nature. For I have the desire to do what is good, but I cannot carry it out. For I do not do the good I want to do, but the evil I do not want to do—this I keep on doing. Now if I do what I do not want to do, it is no longer I who do it, but it is sin living in me that does it. (Romans 7:18-20)

This is the false self at work within us, causing us to act and react in ways contrary to our conscious will. Anger, lust, sloth, image management, the need for control, and of course, the primary sin of pride all come from this place. Thankfully our God is for us, has delivered us, gives to us, justifies for us, intercedes for us, and loves us (Romans 8:31-37).

SOME OF THE LIES OF PRIDE

Undergirding the false self are the lies we tell ourselves. Often subconscious, these unspoken scripts end up driving us throughout our lives, affecting our careers, relationships, and ministries, as well as our relationship with God. See if you can relate to any of these lies of pride.

I am what I do. Your self-worth is tied to achievement. You always feel like you have to perform to be accepted. You're sometimes accused of being a workaholic, but you secretly cling to the label, like it is a compliment. You can be guilted into doing things, and you believe at some level that people won't like you unless you work hard and serve often. So you collect achievements like trophies and use them to justify your worth at some level.

I am who I can successfully pretend to be. Your self-worth is tied to how you're seen. You spend time managing your image, and you worry a lot about how people perceive you. This may manifest itself physically in your appearance, or socially in how you act around others or in how you embrace materialism as a means of posturing. This is the sin of the Pharisees, and it's prevalent in churches that put value on outward appearances or put their pastors on a pedestal.

I'm worthless. Your self-worth is damaged in some way—maybe due to family-of-origin issues or your upbringing or a significant event that scarred you. Low self-esteem is common to many and is extremely deep-seated. It's hard to accept love and grace from others and from God, because you don't believe you're worth it. You may not think that low self-esteem is an issue of pride, but it is, because low self-esteem keeps you focused on yourself and not on God.

I really am all that. Of course, you would never say that out loud. But internally, you believe it. Your self-worth is inflated or at some level augmented. You really believe that your apparent successes, stature, or talents make you better than others. And you have to believe it, because your sense of superiority is the basis of your identity. This is a tough lie to break through, because people who believe this, particularly narcissists, often have an inability to see things from another person's point of view.

The world is a dangerous place. We all have emotional scars, and we learn how to protect ourselves as a result. For some of us, this manifests itself in having control issues, being risk-averse, being socially avoidant or reclusive, or just living in a covert but constant fear. You learned these mechanisms to protect yourself from pain and hurt, but they can also keep you at arm's length from intimacy with God and others.

This all may sound harsh, but we all suffer to some degree from more than one of these lies. Do any of these unspoken scripts play out in your mind? Do they ring out at some subterranean level? These lies—and many others—ultimately come from the Deceiver. Being "transformed by the renewing of your mind" is to reprogram (or rehabituate) ourselves from the lies (Romans 12:2), as well as to embrace the truth of our identity in Christ. Through the Holy Spirit, we must learn to tell the truth about ourselves to ourselves. In this way we can truly worship in the truth, with honesty and fullness.

THE FOUR PERSONAS

One can argue that there are four aspects to your identity—four personas, if you will: (1) who you think you are, (2) who you try to portray yourself to be, (3) who people see when they encounter you, and (4) who God sees.

Who you think you are. We all have a sense of self that defines us, and our actions spring from it. And all of us think things about ourselves that aren't true or at least are skewed from the truth. We have defense mechanisms, identity issues, wrong self-image, family-of-origin issues—all sorts of stuff. These things lead to the dysfunctions that keep us from becoming more like Christ.

For example, someone may grow up having heard over and over that she was stupid. And so, while she may never verbalize it, she constantly hears a voice in her head that tells her so. When she does something wrong, it confirms this wrong self-identity, and this confirmation becomes the trigger to continue the cycle of subconscious self-deprecation. It takes a great deal of self-awareness to break the cycle.

Here's another example: You may believe, at some deep level, that your identity comes from your accomplishments. So you spend your life trying to win awards, trophies, and other achievements to earn the approval of others. (I've found this to be true of many artists and creatives.) This seems to work okay as long as people like what you do. But when people don't like your song, painting, or poem, you believe they must not like you. This thinking is not only skewed, it's also damaging to the soul.

Who you try to portray yourself to be. Who you think you are leads to image management, which is trying to control the way people see you. If you like who you think you are, you'll do things to try to represent that to others. If you don't like who you think you are, you'll do things to hide that from others. The reality for most of us is that we end up doing both. Examples are wearing a certain type of clothes to give off a particular image, writing a blog in the third person, name dropping (by the way, I was talking to Bono once about name dropping), or one of the musician's favorite image management tools: false humility. (I told a person once that he sang a particular song very well. He said with feigned humility, "No, that wasn't me. That was God." I replied honestly, "Actually, no. It wasn't *that* good.")

There's an irony here for those who frequent the platform. As performers who act, sing, speak, or play onstage, we have a public persona that's different from our personal persona. Stage presence is a necessary part of being a performer, and if you're a performing artist of any renown, your stage presence follows you off the stage. So you're trained to manage your image. But your fans end up having a relationship with who they think you are, not who you really are.

Unfortunately image management is no stranger to the church. Many of us have experienced church subcultures in which, in an effort toward authenticity, holiness was replaced by religiosity. Our churches want us to be authentic, but not *that* authentic. They don't want pastors who drink beer, elders who smoke cigars, young people with tats and body piercings, children who run around and make messes, or worship leaders who listen to Lady Gaga. They would rather people act, perform, and be "good Christians" instead of being the imperfectly saved sinners they really are.

All of us—in conscious and subconscious ways—manage our images before others. But that's not necessarily how people see us.

Who people see when they encounter you. Have you ever known someone who was obviously trying to image manage, but it wasn't working? And he didn't have a clue that he was coming off that way? There's a distinct disconnect between who he wanted to appear to be and who he actually came off as. For example, consider the Steve Carell character in the TV series *The Office*. Well, you're that guy. *Everyone* is that guy, to some degree.

The result of image management is that no one sees the image we want them to see. Instead they see a skewed version of that image, which is some combination of what they experience and who we are when no one else is looking. Granted, some of us are better at pretending than others, and some of us are better at discerning people than others, but the result is still the same. We're like a middle-aged man combing over his bald spot—we all walk around with some degree of discernable inauthenticity.

All of this raises the question, Are any of these three identities valid or right? Well, to answer that we need to examine the fourth persona.

Who God sees. Beyond all the other personas is the person God sees. He knows us through and through. He has seen every bit of us—good, bad, and ugly. He's seen every embarrassing moment, every mistake and failure, every soul wound, every concealed sin. And here's the amazing part: he loves us.

God sees more than the bad stuff. He sees the *imago Dei*, the image of God designed into us. And as such, we have infinite and eternal worth in his eyes. So here's the crux of what I'm trying to say: this persona, who *God* sees, is the only one that matters, because this is the only persona that's ultimately true.

So, what does God see in you? What is your real identity in Christ?

You are a child of God, who he dearly loves. You are a member of a chosen race, a people for God's own possession. You are an heir of God. You are a joint heir with Christ, sharing in his inheritance. You are righteous and holy, set apart for God's purposes and for his glory. You are an expression of the very life of Christ. You are his workmanship, in whom God's love is being perfected, God's beloved. (Find these truths in John 1:12; 1 Peter 2:9-10; Galatians 4:6; Romans 8:17; Ephesians 2:10; 4:24; Colossians 3:4; 1 John 2:5; 4:12; 4:17.)

This is the person God sees in you. This is the persona that's eternally real. This is your true identity, completely stripped of pride. So why hold on to the false identities when true humility in God gives you an identity that's so much better, richer, deeper, truer?

EMBRACING AUTHENTICITY

The reality is that authenticity isn't that easy. I've met many people who—because of their baggage and complex systems of self-deception—have a hard time breaking through to the real self. If the soul were a garden, there are parts overgrown, swampy, and dark. It takes a lot of courage to walk into those dark parts of our soul and start pulling weeds.

Here's an uncommon definition of *authenticity*: the act of aligning all of your personas so they're all congruent. So the person you think you are is the person you project to others, which is the person people actually see, which is the person God sees—the true self.

I began to see some of these things in myself through the revelation of the Holy Spirit, the grace extended by people around me, and imperfect but diligent discipline. I began to see that I had unknowingly attached my identity to my roles as a pastor and leader and "recording artist" (whatever that means) in very unhealthy ways. I began to understand that God didn't need me to accomplish big things for him in order to be loved. I didn't need to get my way in order to bolster my self-image. I didn't need to protect myself from criticism, which was mostly well-meaning, constructive, and helpful.

Over time—and through diligent rehabituation of my thoughts and actions—it became easier and easier for me to let go. God didn't need my songs, my talents, my words, my ambitions. Eventually these things became an act of love to God, not a means to try to be accepted by him. As I let go of my false self, I no longer struggled with and fought against things that were incongruent to it. I could simply be me. And that was good enough.

The eleventh chapter of Matthew records Jesus beginning to preach to the towns of Galilee. He revealed his role as the Son of God, and he offered them an invitation to a better way:

> Are you tired? Worn out? Burned out on religion? Come to me. Get away with me and you'll recover your life. I'll show you how to take a real rest. Walk with me and work with me—watch how I do it. Learn the unforced rhythms of grace. I won't lay anything heavy or ill-fitting on you. Keep

company with me and you'll learn to live freely and lightly. (Matthew 11:28-30 *The Message*)

I believe Jesus was saying, in part, that you can let go of all those systems of religiosity and self-deception, the false devices of approval and acceptance, the lies people told you about yourself that you believed, the belief that you can earn worth and salvation. All these things oppress, deceive, and wound the soul. Instead, you can know the Father through a living and vibrant relationship with the Son, a relationship in which you know he knows every part of you—warts and all—and loves you fully (Matthew 11:27).

The issue of identity is fundamental to our growth as followers of Christ. It's foundational to our understanding of humility— truly knowing who we are before God. And it's central to our ability to worship "in the Spirit and in truth" (John 4:23-24). For to be true to yourself, to your friends, to the world, and to God, you must understand who you really are.

WORSHIP PRACTICE

Review some of the lies of pride listed in this chapter, and carefully and prayerfully consider what lies are at the foundation of the things you do, the thoughts you think, the way you live. Do any of these lies have power over you? Is there a hidden narrative that your brain subconsciously continues to tell you, keeping you from the fullness of God's love? Where does that come from? Why do you believe it?

Now here's the hard part: Identify a person you trust who has spiritual maturity and the gift of discernment. In the safety of complete confidentiality and trust, share this narrative with that person. Christian fellowship is a sacred thing in that God is in our midst when we are with other believers. In the sacredness of fellowship with this other person—a sacredness built on trust and confidentiality—honestly and bravely share your story.

Five

WORSHIP FROM THE TRUE SELF

> If we walk in the light, as he is in the light, we
> have fellowship with one another, and the blood
> of Jesus, his Son, purifies us from all sin.
>
> 1 JOHN 1:7

"**PLEASE PLACE YOUR IDS** on the counter."

The correctional officer was professional but impersonal, which didn't allay my anxiety. We had just arrived, and already I was beginning to question whether this was a good idea. My band had been invited by a prison ministry to perform a concert and lead worship for their two Sunday services at an area correctional facility. The slammer, the pokey, the big house—everyone has preconceived notions about prison. Mine were colored by grim, gritty movies like *The Shawshank Redemption* and *The Green Mile*. So I had more than a little trepidation.

When my band checked in at the main building, staff carefully frisked us and inventoried our equipment and cords before ushering us through two security doors and into the inner courtyard.

The guard tower was a silent, steady reminder that this was no ordinary gig. We set up our drums, guitars, and keyboard on the chapel stage. Several convicts milled around us, all wearing powder blue shirts and jeans, and offered their assistance. They were friendly, helpful. They were just like you and me.

Soon the well-worn pews of the chapel were filled to capacity. And at the first downbeat we were off. These men worshiped! They sang loud and clapped hard and raised their hands with heartfelt spontaneity. They overtly encouraged us to lead them. They responded with conviction and certainty and abandon. It was like they really believed the God of the universe was in this chapel with them. Because he was.

The second service that afternoon was filled to overflowing, mostly with new inmates who had heard about the morning session. And it was even more lively. "Off the hook!" our ministry leader, Greg, described it. "The best response I've ever seen." The ninety-minute service ran an extra hour, and finally, after playing every song we had twice, I finally had to admit to the men that we had run out of prepared music.

"Sing 'Amazing Grace'!" one of the men shouted. So we did. And it was. Amazing.

The response was nothing short of supernatural. Grown men falling to their knees and on their faces, crying and singing and coming forward for prayer. Thirty inmates came forward at the altar call, with others coming to meet them. It was extraordinary to see these men, tattooed and hardened by stories unspoken, completely unraveled by God, completely unashamed of their need for his mercy and forgiveness. In these holy moments, I had the privilege of experiencing these men stripped and released of the pretense of their false selves, giving themselves honestly and fully to God.

One thing became tangibly real to me that afternoon: these men knew about God's grace in ways that I did not. And they didn't take that grace for granted. In a very real way, it was all they had. For many of us grace is seemingly wrapped up in our busy, privileged lives and our egocentric, false pretensions. But behind concrete walls and barbed-wire fences, words like *repentance, mercy, freedom,* and *truth* took on deeper meanings.

In my reflections later, it occurred to me that I'm not so different from the people behind those prison bars. I once was lost but now am found. My need for grace, for unraveling, for reconciliation, for God, is just the same. For true freedom can only be found in Christ. Only in Christ can we know the truth, and only in Christ can the truth set us truly free (John 8:32).

IN THE SPIRIT AND IN TRUTH

Early in his ministry, Jesus and his disciples were traveling through Samaria and found themselves just outside the small, dusty town of Sychar (John 4). His followers went into the village to barter for some food, so Jesus, looking for a place to rest, found a lonely spot at Jacob's well. Tired and thirsty, he saw a Samaritan woman at the well, and he violated social custom by engaging in conversation with her. It was a simple request: "Will you give me a drink?" (John 4:7).

In their ensuing exchange, Jesus corrected the Samaritan woman on some wrong thinking regarding God and worship. The obvious correction was when Jesus explained the truth of who God really is, saying that the Samaritans "worship what you do not know" (John 4:22). But in the larger context of their conversation

Jesus offered another necessary truth—the truth of who the Samaritan woman was. He explained, "God is spirit, and his worshipers must worship in the Spirit and in truth" (John 4:24). This is honest worship, worship from the true self.

Jesus revealed to the woman that she was living a life of deceit, deceiving herself even as she tried to image-manage herself. He gently exposed her lies about her previous marriages and relationships and lovingly unraveled her false self. (We can infer that their conversation was much longer than recorded in the Bible, because she later said in verse 29 he had told her everything she had ever done.) Rather than criticizing and condemning, Jesus uncloaked her pretense in a way that was life giving and filled with hope.

Finally he offered her one more truth: the truth of his being. "I, the one speaking to you—I am he" (John 4:26). It was a beautiful interchange between the two of them, Jesus reaching out not only beyond the postures of social class but also beyond the postures of the woman's false self. And it changed the woman forever.

One of the unspoken realities of our Sunday-morning gatherings is that we worship in a truth that's clouded by our false selves. This makes sense, as we perceive through the clouded lenses of the firmly entrenched pretenses and mechanisms that exist in our false selves. Since we relate to the entire universe through the structure of our false selves, our connection to God is filtered and distorted as well.

When we worship in this way, we aren't worshiping from who we're intended to be. From this false self, we not only deceive ourselves, we also offer our pretense to God. Remember our operating definition of humility: truly knowing who we are before God. This is the key to what it means to worship in the Spirit and in truth—to worship in the truth of who God is with the truth of who we are. This is one of the reasons unwrapping the false self is so very important. God desires honest worship from a place of wholeness, devoid of our dysfunctions and self-distortions, where we're truly free to worship spirit to Spirit. This is self-awareness in light of God-awareness, the true God worshiped by the true self. It's worshiping with God-bathed humility, for he knows our brokenness, our weakness, our sin. And he not only loves and accepts us, he also desires that we become whole in the process.

But it isn't that easy. Those of us who have father wounds have trouble worshiping a God who describes himself as the perfect Father. Those of us who have image management issues are emotionally unable to admit fully the ugliness of our sins before the God who is holy, holy, holy. Those of us who have intimacy issues can't fully enter into the vulnerable intimacy of a loving God or of his faith community. Those of us with poor self-image or low self-esteem issues may find ourselves never fully accepting and receiving grace. Those burdened by false guilt have a hard time shedding the need to be self-punishing and simply accepting God's perfect forgiveness. And those of us who have grown up in a shame-based family or culture find it hard to live freely and fully in the joy of the Lord. These are some of the ways in which our spiritual formation (or deformation) is tied deeply to worship.

But our gracious God is bigger than the things that keep us from him. He is the one who tore the veil that separated us (Luke 23:45). God *is* the perfect Father. He *is* the Holy One. He *is* intimate and loving. His forgiveness covers all sins, and his grace is fully available to all. And God desires that we all live freely and fully and honestly in his joy.

I've met some people who, when presented with the concepts of false self and true self, shrug their shoulders and respond with this: "This may be needed for a few people, but generally, isn't this unnecessary? I mean, we're washed in the blood, aren't we? Aren't our sins already forgiven?" While it's true that our sins are forgiven, the very question reveals a truncated, transactional understanding of the gospel. The gospel isn't just Jesus on the cross. It's also Jesus now and forever. Indeed, the gospel is more than just the forgiveness of our sins and salvation of our souls for heaven. It includes the invitation to walk with Jesus through the Spirit on a path toward freedom from dysfunction and fear and shame and self-deception, a path toward wholeness, honesty, and joy. We take our wholeness, or lack of it, to heaven with us. It isn't just the starting line; it's the entire race. This is the path that leads to Spirit and truth in our worship.

FREEDOM FROM THE LIES

One of the main reasons I found it difficult to dig my way through my junk and begin to uncover my true self was because I'm very good at self-deception, as we all are. We're all good at hiding ourselves from ourselves. Dr. Gerald May stated, "We become addicted to our own self-images. Our cellular representations of self habituate, adapt, and control us. . . . As with other addictions, we do not readily relinquish our attachments to self-images. In fact, we may cling to them more tenaciously than to any other attachments."[1]

We all have a lifetime of training ourselves into thinking we're a certain kind of person, and there's much risk in admitting we may not see ourselves truthfully. It's risky because if we discover that we aren't who we think we are, who are we really? Such discoveries can lead to a crisis of identity, a crisis of relationships, even a crisis of faith.

This is one reason being in a faith community is so important. We need people with whom we can share our internal struggles, pains, and self-talk, people who can sift through our stuff and help us see ourselves more clearly. If you don't think you have a problem with self-deception, ask someone with the gift of discernment to tell you the truth about who you are. If you don't have people who will speak the truth to you, you need to find them. And here's the hardest part: When you find those people, listen to them. In humility, assume that you don't know or see what they see and that some part of what they see about you reveals your self-deceptions.

In the midst of one particularly harried day, a friend stopped me and remarked, "Is that the way your shirt is made? It looks inside out." And it was true. I was in such a hurry that morning that I failed to notice I had put on my T-shirt the wrong way. I realized that many people had seen me like this but never mentioned it to me. Thankfully I had one friend who was willing to tell me the truth about my wardrobe.

The false self is that place where we camouflage and self-deceive, but also where we minimize and even justify our sinfulness. Though we profess Christ, love God, and are generally good people, many of us still carry secret sins in our baggage. A man may carry with him a secret addiction to pornography that manifests itself in web browsing. A woman may carry a lifelong but unspoken envy of a sister that displays itself in passive-aggression. A man may have anger issues, lashing out at his wife and children in private, yet presenting a blissful family life outside the walls of their home. A well-established churchgoer may find herself comfortable in her self-made piety and find that each Sunday morning only confirms her spiritual superiority over others.

Remember, many of the motivations behind our secret sins have their roots in the false self. We haven't learned how to trust God for our joy and happiness, so we self-medicate through private thoughts and private actions. We turn to our secret sins—which are addictions to our wrong emotional programming—in an attempt to protect us from the world and make us happy. Like the woman at the well, we try to deceive God with the exterior parts of our lives. But in the process, we only deceive ourselves.

The truth is, only by shining light on our secret sins can we have any hope for real happiness. Just as Jesus shined his light into the Samaritan woman (and that light changed her perception of herself and of the Messiah), we must have the courage to allow others into the dark places of our lives. And we must allow Jesus there most of all.

WORSHIPING FROM THE TRUE SELF

So, what does it look like to worship from the true self? Let me offer you a definition: The true self is the person we can become when God is free to manifest himself through our God-given uniqueness. God designed us as unique individuals, and he doesn't want to take that away from us. On the contrary, finding our true self allows our distinctiveness to thrive, to be more freely expressed, so we can more freely worship. It is the full and honest expression of who we are. The apostle John reminds us,

"If we walk in the light, as he is in the light, we have fellowship with one another, and the blood of Jesus, his Son, purifies us from all sin" (1 John 1:7).

When we worship from our true self, we aren't distracted by wrong thoughts about ourselves or others, not led by wrong emotions or feelings, not sidetracked from the idle chatter that floats in the backs of our brains during times of worship. When we worship from the true self, we're open to a deeper relationship with the community of the Godhead—Father, Son, and Spirit—as well as with the community of the church. When we worship from the true self, the Holy Spirit has greater freedom to speak into us, and us to him. When we worship from the true self, we can see God more clearly, without the distortions that come from our self-concepts or wrong thoughts. When we worship from the true self, humility is the natural posture of our souls. We can live honestly and fully. We are actually transformed (Romans 12:2).

As I write these words, I'm struck again by how difficult it can be to work through these issues. It's like diving into the dark blackness of the deepest ocean, not knowing what lurks at the bottom—or not even knowing how to use the scuba gear. Add to that powerful external issues such as living in a consumer-driven, spectacle-oriented, and narcissistic society. Our culture is steeped in materialism and hedonism, esteems superficiality and appearance over substance and character, is self-seeking and self-adoring. The culture overwhelms us into clinging to and building up our false selves in a hundred different ways.

My story includes hundreds of hours talking with good and trusted friends, time with a discerning therapist, reading insightful Christian books, and prayerfully applying spiritual disciplines and worship practices. It includes coming to grips with the fact that I'm not who I thought I was, but realizing that I can indeed become the person God intends me to be. And above all, I can cling to the truth that I'm a son of the King, dearly beloved of the Father. It was, at times, frustrating, depressing, and even scary. But over time and with attentiveness, the Spirit of God has been dismantling my false self and making me something new.

You see, God intends that life in the kingdom be lived in right relationship with Jesus. This God-filled life is characterized by right thoughts, feelings, habits, and choices. Honest worship requires the true self in right relationship with the true God. It is worship as God intended—in the Spirit and in truth.

BURNING BUSHES

The Moses who crashed the stone tablets and made the Hebrews smelt down the golden calf was a far cry from the Moses who sought anonymity and refuge in the desert. The Moses who fled Egypt to Midian, the Hebrew who was the adopted son of Pharaoh's daughter, the royal who became a shepherd was formed by a critical event: an encounter with a burning bush.

The scene unfolds in the third chapter of Exodus. Moses was tending the flocks of his father-in-law at Horeb, the mountain of God. There he encountered God through a vision of a bush blazing with an unquenchable fire. As he approached this visage, he heard the voice of God calling him by name, and responded,

"Here I am."

"Do not come any closer," God said. "Take off your sandals, for the place where you are standing is holy ground." Then he said, "I am the God of your father, the God of Abraham, the God of Isaac and the God of Jacob." At this, Moses hid his face, because he was afraid to look at God. (Exodus 3:4-6)

The God of his forefathers inserted himself unmistakably into Moses' life, and his first response was to hide his face. Undoubtedly he was fearful of the almighty power of God. But I think there was more to it. He was awestruck by God's holiness and also his own inadequacies in light of that holiness. Not coincidentally, this is the same response Adam and Eve had after they ate from the tree (Genesis 3:6-11). And we can't blame Moses for this. He had a lot of baggage to carry—years of shame and guilt from the secret sin of his murderous act, estrangement and fear from being a refugee and fugitive, and some world-class family-of-origin issues (Exodus 2:1-10).

The conversation that followed bears this out. God had a plan for Moses to be used as an instrument for the rescue of his people. But Moses had excuses. *What if I'm not adequate? What if they don't believe me? What if I don't speak well?* Moses was still living under the oppression of his false self, not fully realizing that his success wouldn't come from himself but from God. Moses did not yet comprehend the lies he believed about himself—his inadequacies, his failings, his guilt. Nor had he learned the truth about himself that comes from God. He didn't yet understand that our God is a God who rescues and redeems individuals and people from bondage—physical, emotional, and spiritual.

But Moses did eventually understand the heart of God and his special place in it. From Egypt to Midian, from the Red Sea to Mount Sinai, from the Sinai wilderness to the Jordan River, God slowly but surely transformed Moses. God was able to use him as an instrument to save the children of Israel—from bondage to freedom, from chains to the threshold of the Promised Land.

Perhaps the first step to finding your true self is simply taking off your sandals. God invited Moses into the light of his presence and declared it holy ground. Living a life in lordship to Christ means constantly living on this holy ground, allowing God to shed his light into the corners and crevices of who we are. We're exposed and undone in his presence, and though at times we may protest, God works graciously to change us and mold us and make us new.

WORSHIP PRACTICE

Silence and solitude are two classic spiritual disciplines that have been practiced over the centuries. They require the ability to be alone somewhere for an extended period, to be silent in contemplation and prayer. This is much more than just a physical exercise. We must be able to silence the clatter in our minds and open the eyes of our hearts to see God.

Take a full day or weekend away by yourself, if you can, to connect with God. Specifically try to have a "woman at the well" encounter with God, where you ask him to reveal the hidden parts of your false self. Don't put too much on your agenda, and do turn off your electronic devices. Just sit before God in silence and in solitude for an extended length of time. Jot down your thoughts throughout your time, and later share them with a close and trusted friend.

Six

SOUL WORSHIP

Bless the LORD, O my soul,
And all that is within me, bless His holy name.

PSALM 103:1 NASB

IN THE MOVIE *O Brother, Where Art Thou?* protagonist Ulysses McGill picks up a mysterious hitchhiker determined to be a recording star. In the course of their conversation, Tommy Johnson reveals that he had just recently sold his soul to the devil. Curious, Ulysses asks Tommy, "What'd the devil give you for your soul, Tommy?"

Tommy answers, "Well, he taught me to play this here guitar real good."

Ulysses's cohort, Delmar O'Donnell, is shocked. "Oh, son. For that you sold your everlasting soul?"

Tommy's reply is misguided but honest. "Well," he says, "I wasn't usin' it."

We tend to refer to the soul a lot. We talk about playing with soul, expressing from our soul, putting our heart and soul into our passions. We sing songs about our souls, to our souls, from our souls. There is soul food, soul music, soul sisters, soul catchers, soulmates, soul patches, even chicken soup for the soul. We understand implicitly that *soul* refers to something mysterious, eternal, and deeply rooted in the very essence of who we are. By inference, we also implicitly understand that the soul is deeply related to worship. But there is much misunderstanding. If pressed toward a fuller explanation of the soul, I'm afraid most everyone would be unable to come up with a theologically robust definition. Nonetheless, I believe that an understanding of the soul can be very helpful as we explore a more expansive expression of worship.

SOUL SEARCHING

In his book *Renovation of the Heart*, Dallas Willard posits that the soul "is that dimension of the person that interrelates all of the other dimensions so that they form one life."[1] He goes on to describe the soul as containing spirit (heart/will), mind, social context, and body. This description of the soul struck me as both theologically sound and simple to understand. When I started to apply this model to my understanding of worship, I became more and more convinced that a better understanding of the soul is essential to worship.

According to Willard, the soul can be described as a series of concentric circles. And by implication, these parts of us are not fragmented, partitioned pieces but are nested aspects of one whole.

In the center circle is our heart or will, the human capacity to choose. Our intentions, judgments, and decisions spring from this nucleus. This makes sense, as our will is at the crux of our relationship with God. In contrast to the more secular, romantic view, Willard contends that the term *heart* has a fuller and more biblical meaning—as the core of an individual, that part "where decisions and choices are made for the whole person." Free will is the great gift—the ability to choose dominion over our self or to surrender it comes from this place.

Moving from the center outward, the second concentric circle is the mind. This includes our thoughts, memories, emotions, values, and conscience. Habits (good and bad) and ways of thinking (good and bad) are created here, and it's where we create personal preferences and discover our individuality. It should be acknowledged that the terms *heart* and *mind* can get muddled when mentioned in the Bible. Obviously the Bible often speaks metaphorically, not anatomically, when using these words.

The next concentric circle is our body—our physicality in the universe—which gives us the ability to act on our will and mind. This circle includes everything from eating, sleeping, hugging, dancing, painting, and doing the dishes to body language and facial expressions. These make it possible for us to interact with others and with the created universe.

It's important to note that we don't have a body and a soul; our body is a part of our soul. Contrary to some movies or Bugs Bunny cartoons, your body doesn't just house your soul; your body is part of the integration of your soul. And that makes sense if you think about how the chemical makeup of our bodies and brains is highly interconnected with our feelings and thinking; our flesh is connected to our emotions and attitudes.[2]

Now we can begin to define the soul. Willard states, "The soul is the capacity to integrate all the parts into a single, whole life." John Ortberg described this further:

Your soul is what integrates your will (your intentions), your mind (your thoughts and feelings, your values and conscience), and your body (your face, body language, and actions) into a single life. A soul is healthy—well-ordered—when there is harmony between these three entities and God's intention for all creation. When you are connected with God and other people in life, you have a healthy soul.[3]

There are many implications, both large and small, with this understanding of the soul. The soul is more than just the sum of the parts. At its best, it's also the integration or alignment of the whole self in harmony to God and his will. We're intended to be fully integrated—our will, mind, and body aligned with our self, with others, with creation, and with God. This is why it's so important to understand, and hopefully dismantle, the false self—it undermines the integration of our souls. This is why sin is such an invader—it poisons and misaligns our souls. This is why Spirit and truth are essential aspects of worship—worship is intended to be our aligned souls also aligned to the Spirit of God. This is the well-ordered life that we desperately and innately desire. And God desires this for us as well.

Unfortunately, we tend to live dis-integrated lives in which our will and our mind and even our body are at odds. The surrender of our wills and renewing of our minds are counterintuitive to the world, so we devote ourselves to many wrong activities, tell ourselves lies about ourselves and our motives, and spend much too much time on image management. We create sophisticated defense mechanisms and medicate ourselves with wrong activities and things. We fall into addictions, large and small, that affect our wills, our minds, and our bodies. We're more easily swayed by the fame, narcissism, self-seeking pleasures, and mind-numbing addictions than we'd ever admit. We don't understand that "being saved" really means being formed into an integrated soul—from false to true self—living in a way that is fully aligned with God's intentions for us.

Why is understanding the soul important? Because it's central to Jesus' implied definition of worship.

HEART AND SOUL AND MIND AND STRENGTH

During the course of his earthly teaching, Jesus had many opponents and detractors. His words disrupted the social and political orders, as he invited us to a better way, a kingdom-oriented way. In Matthew 22, several sects were trying to trap Jesus with their rhetoric. In the midst of a heated conversation, a pharisaical lawyer baited Jesus with the question, "Which is the greatest commandment?" Though he was trying to expose Jesus for his lack of knowledge, Jesus didn't hesitate with the perfect, definitive answer. He quotes the Torah, from the book of Deuteronomy: "'Love the Lord your God with all your heart and with all your soul and with all your mind.' This is the first and greatest commandment" (Matthew 22:37-38).[4]

There are many good definitions of worship. And one of my favorite descriptions of worship comes from these words of Jesus, which capture not only the great commandment but also the essence of what worship is. Worship is an expression of love. And love happens within the context of a relationship. God loves us. He reveals that love to us. And we respond to that love by loving him back with our songs, with our prayers, and with the way we live our lives. Jesus reveals that our loving God loves us with all that he is and desires all that we are.

I concur with Dr. Bruce Leafblad that "worship is the highest form of love."[5] So, as a thought experiment, let's exchange the word *love* with the word *worship* in the passage: "You shall worship the Lord your God with all your heart and with all your soul and with all your mind and with all your strength."

We worship him with our hearts, from the core of who we are. We worship willfully and purposefully as an expression of our identity in Christ, from our true self. And we worship with an emotional love, for our God is an emotional God. He grieves for us when we grieve and celebrates with us when we celebrate, and his joy permeates this universe.

We also worship him with our minds, our intellects, grounded in the Word of God, able to understand and discern his truth and apply it in a way that's meaningful and life-changing. Worshiping God is a mindful act involving our thoughts and meditations, our memories and emotions, our values and beliefs, and our conscience and convictions. We know the will of God, as well as God himself, in great part through our minds.

We also worship with our strength. We worship with expressions of our body, with musical instruments, with singing, with raising our hands and bowing our heads. And we also worship in strength through acts of service, acts of sacrifice, acts of putting others first and ourselves last by loving our neighbors and reaching out to the disenfranchised and the broken. In a sense, worship is incarnated—embodied in flesh— through our physical bodies. These are all acts of worship that require our strength.

This is what it is to have the soul of a worshiper, to worship with heart and mind and body. To worship with the totality of who we are. Willard adds, "When we are like this, our whole life is an eternal one. Everything we do counts for eternity and is preserved there (Colossians 3:17)."[6] We're invited into a full life that's not our own, to live joyously and abundantly in his kingdom, a reality that's greater than what we can see. Our God desires us to live fully soul-integrated lives, and he also desires that our worship come from fully integrated souls.

That's why a proper understanding of the soul is important to worship. Think about the most transcendent and inspired moment of worship you've had. Most likely, it occurred in a time of total engagement, when you had surrendered your whole self to worshiping God. In such moments, our worship is an activity that allows our will (intentions), mind (emotions, passions, intellect), and body (physicality)—the totality of our soul—to align to God. These are the deep, ethereal convergences of heaven and earth when we feel most fully alive, times when worship feels like brokenness and wholeness, surrender and freedom, all at the same time. I'm becoming more and more convinced that this is a taste of heaven, when our soul is fully aligned to itself, to God, to all creation.

Now a disclaimer. These passages in Deuteronomy and in Matthew aren't meant to be an anatomy lesson, describing heart, soul, mind, and strength as discrete parts of a person. They are much more interconnected and blurred than that. We are made in the image of God, not as simple parts strung together but as complex, interconnected, wondrous beings. What we believe, what we feel, what we experience, and how God meets us in that are all connected somehow in some mysterious and God-breathed ways.

We use the words *heart, soul, mind,* and *strength* in conceptual and blurry ways, and so does the Bible. So don't get caught up in the definitions. We can safely assume that when Jesus used the words *heart, soul,* and *mind,* he meant for us to love God with all that we are, the entirety of our being.

SOUL WORSHIP

Hopefully, applying this simple understanding of the soul, together with Jesus' great commandment, as a working definition of worship gives us a more complete understanding of the very special privilege and calling of worship. Soul worship is the integral fullness of heart, soul, mind, and strength to love God. But is that the worship we experience when we gather on Sunday morning?

In some traditions, there's a tendency to believe that worship is primarily an emotive act. And while emotion is important, emotion unchecked has the potential to devolve into irrationality. Other faith streams believe that emotion isn't to be emphasized, so worship has the potential to devolve into an intellectual act. Some are inhibited from physical displays of worship, and their reservations can hold back important bodily expressions of praise. Those who are loud, hand-raising, hand-clapping worshipers can learn from the expressions of silence and solitude. Soul worship is the entirety and integration of heart and soul and mind and strength—every part of who we are—offered up in love and full devotion to the King. As worshipers, that should be our highest aspiration.

So, what does soul worship look like in the Bible? It is King David amid the shouts and the fanfare of trumpets, leaping and dancing before the procession as the ark of the Lord was brought into the city of his name. He described his soul worship as being "even more undignified than this" (2 Samuel 6:22).

Soul worship is Isaiah overwhelmed at the sight of the glory of God—high and exalted and seated on his throne—crying out as an offering, "Here am I. Send me!" (Isaiah 6:1-8).

Soul worship is Mary, face to face with an angel of the Lord, quietly offering up her heart and mind and body with the words, "I am the Lord's servant. . . . May your word to me be fulfilled" (Luke 1:38).

Soul worship is the woman with the alabaster jar, pouring perfume worth a year's wages on the head of Jesus. Overcome by grace, her quiet act of love was bold and extravagant, and it foreshadowed the bold and extravagant act of the cross (Mark 14:3-10).

Soul worship is the voices of the ten thousand times ten thousand who encircle the throne and exclaim, "Worthy is the Lamb, who was slain!" and every creature in heaven and on earth singing,

> To him who sits on the throne and to the Lamb
> be praise and honor and glory and power,
> for ever and ever! (Revelation 5:1-14)

AN ACT OF THE WILL

In this more complete picture of worship—involving heart, soul, mind, and strength—it's important to note that the fundamental driving force behind our worship is the core circle: the will. To discuss this, I'll use the analogy of the wedding ceremony.

I've been a part of probably a hundred weddings. In all weddings, the climax of the ceremony is the sacred exchange of vows. I have a continuing practice: whenever the vows are exchanged, I always restate the vows in my head to my wife as a renewing of my commitment to her. I've probably said my wedding vows over a hundred times over the past few decades. I think it's important to remind myself occasionally of the things I've committed to, to my wife and before God.

When you declare your marriage vows to your spouse, you don't vow to fall in love. You vow to love, honor, and cherish. In other words, love is more than an emotion. It's an act of the will. Think about that. God commands us to love one another, and even our enemies, which is obviously not an emotional love but an act of the will. Certainly love is an emotion, but faithfulness redefines love to be much more than that. It's also a decision, an act of selflessness, something we express even when we don't feel like it.

So we choose to love our spouse, our parents, our children, our neighbor, or our enemy even when we don't feel like it. That's because the choice is as much an act of love as the love itself. That's what real love is.

Do you see why this is important? I sometimes hear people say they aren't in the mood to enter into corporate worship. Singing is "not me," they say. Since they don't feel like singing, they decide it would be more honest not to participate in corporate worship. Or they feel that raising their hands or clapping is forced or disingenuous, so they think it's more honest to leave their arms hanging. I do understand that worship requires self-examination, integrity, and wholeheartedness. But it's also true that God is worthy of us raising hands, worthy of our song, worthy of "alabaster jar" expressions that may be out of our comfort zones (Matthew 26:6-13).

There's an inherent danger in equating worship with feelings, and many of us have been in situations where our feelings were manipulated. We've all heard stories of churches where worship was fervent and seemingly alive, but behind the scenes, the people didn't live like they knew the God they worshiped. You see, if all we focus on is the emotive sincerity of our worship, we can disregard the larger issue of living the life of a worshiper. Once again, it's choosing experiences of worship over being a worshiper. Feelings are extremely important; feelings can also be wrong. When we equate worship only with feelings, we've made the definition of worship—and the definition of love—too small.

Soul worship begins with a choice, an act of the will. So it matters little if we're in the mood or not. It doesn't matter whether we like the style or the song or the tempo. All of that is subservient to giving God glory because he is worthy. All of that is subservient to the purpose of meeting God and responding to the truth of his story, to his action and presence in our lives. This is a subtle but important distinction. Instead of waiting for the worship leader or the rock band or the pipe organ to rev us up emotionally for worship, we *choose* to worship—assuming a posture of obedience and surrender—as an act of our will. Then we can more honestly allow the Holy Spirit to stir us up emotionally. Emotions are important, but emotions should follow the will, not the other way around.

At this point, it's good to remember that we're mortal, time-bound, circumstantial beings. In other words, each of us is on a journey that includes a life context. When we gather on a Sunday morning, we gather with the man struggling with depression, the single mother trying to make ends meet, the teenager falling in love, the returning veteran trying to reintegrate in society. We bring our circumstances into our worship. As we endeavor to give God our soul worship, we come from the place we are, knowing that God will meet us there.

LIVING OUT OUR WORSHIP

As mentioned earlier, Jesus was quoting Deuteronomy 6 when he responded to the question of what the greatest commandment is. But the context of this passage implies something more expansive. Reading deeper into the passage, we are to love God continually, "when you walk along the road, when you lie down and when you get up. Tie them as symbols on your hands and bind them on your foreheads. Write them on the doorframes of your houses and on your gates" (Deuteronomy 6:7-9). In other words, loving God isn't just an action or something we feel. This is the way we're intended to live: Our love for God permeates everything, soaking into our lives like water into a sponge. It isn't limited to a particular day of the week or a particular time of that day. It's supposed to infuse everything we do and everything we are.

This makes sense when we understand that God designed us to be worshipers. Our souls are designed to be worship-centric, to worship along the road and when we lie down and when we get up. We are created "to glorify God and enjoy him forever."[7]

The integration of the soul—and the worship that springs from it—naturally extends into the living out of our lives. What we do springs from who we are. Soul worship extends to every aspect of our being.

Many years ago, I had just begun serving as the worship pastor for a wonderful church, and it was important that I win over the skeptics, particularly those who preferred a traditional style of worship. When I was asked to speak and lead worship at a senior event, I knew I had to put my best foot forward. I had prepared what I felt was a theologically grounded and engaging sermon, and I stacked the worship set that morning with my favorite hymns. Just to give me an edge, I invited my wife to bring our two incredibly sweet and cuddly four-year-old daughters, Rachel and Paige. I mean, the cute factor couldn't hurt, right?

By the time we arrived, the fellowship hall was already packed, filled primarily with retirees, traditional and proper and quite Baptist. True to form, my daughters began making the rounds, smiling and waving and basically creating delight everywhere they went. I went about the business of pastoring, greeting everyone and making sure everyone felt welcomed and included. But the truth of the matter was, I was the new guy, not them. After some preliminaries, I was invited to step forward and lead them in worship.

As I said, my worship set was stacked with hymns in an effort to connect with this demographic slice of my new congregation. I sat at the grand piano, read a psalm as a call to worship, and invited them to worship with me. Things were going extremely well into the second song. People seemed engaged and were singing robustly, and I was genuinely enjoying those moments before the Lord. What I didn't know was that one of my daughters had slipped away from my wife and made her way onto the stage.

Sensing something odd, I looked up and noticed her in front of the piano, hands in the air, spring dress twirling, feet swirling in lazy circles. Dancing. Elated, her twin sister quickly joined her. And suddenly I had two little ballerinas on the stage.

Now, when I said these people were Baptist, I mean it in the cultural sense of the word. Dancing is akin to gambling, smoking, drinking, playing the lottery, shooting heroin. So I panicked. As a cold sweat broke down the back of my neck, I glanced at my wife, who could only offer me a wide-eyed shrug. I thought about stopping the song and grabbing the girls, but that would have only punctuated the situation.

I am so in trouble, I thought. Resigned to my fate, I kept singing.

In the midst of my panic, I spied the crowd. By this time, most everyone had stopped singing, and I was prepared for the worst. But what I saw nearly stopped me in my tracks. Instead of stern disapproval, I saw a room full of warm, wide smiles. To my surprise, every person there had become captivated by this pair of tiny dancers. The freedom and abandonment they had in expressing their simple joy and delight before God was, in a word, intoxicating.

I continued to sing. "Then sings my soul, my Savior God to Thee, how great Thou art, how great Thou art." And as they twirled and flitted and swept their little arms about, I began to realize that I wasn't leading worship. My daughters were.

Rachel and Paige taught me something that morning: we are made to be worshipers. Without the artificial social constraints that we adults put on ourselves, they were free to express honest worship with the entirety of who they were—heart and mind and soul and strength. And they showed me that God takes great delight in the purely offered worship of his children. I could see it in the way they danced and in the smiles of all who delighted in them.

In the smiles, I felt God shining down on us.

WORSHIP PRACTICE

Do you tend to be reserved and quiet during corporate worship, or are you physically demonstrative? Do you worship primarily with your intellect or with your emotions? Do you come to the service and wait to be ushered into worship, or do you come motivated and ready? What would fully integrated worship look like to you? During your corporate worship experiences, focus on the aspects of mind, will, soul, and strength that aren't your natural inclination. It may include raising your hands high or singing loudly when you typically don't, or working harder at minimizing distractions, or being still. The point is to worship with all your soul circles.

Seven

WHEN THE CHURCH GATHERS

Praise God in the great congregation;
praise the LORD in the assembly of Israel.

PSALM 68:26

ONE OF THE THINGS I look forward to every year is our family holiday meals: Thanksgiving, Christmas, and Easter. Turkey, gravy, mashed potatoes, cranberry sauce—all I have to do is think about it and close my eyes, and I smell my mother-in-law's gravy.

What makes the family holiday meal so special? More than just food. There are a number of elements that we literally bring to the table. We *gather* as a family—immediate and extended, young and old, rich and poor, normal and not-so-normal—and in our diversity we share invisible bonds of fellowship. We're related by blood, so no one is left out.

We acknowledge the *artistry* of the event—the beautiful table setting, the delicious aromas wafting from the kitchen, the festive decorations, and the Christmas music playing in the background. In this atmosphere, there's an anticipation that something very special and meaningful is happening.

As we sit around, we share family *stories*, good and bad, funny and poignant: that hilarious incident that happened to Uncle Joe, the time Aunt Jane burned the turkey, the year Brother Ron was serving overseas and couldn't make it, the births and graduations and other milestones of the clan. Some of these stories are told and retold every Thanksgiving and Christmas and Easter, but no one minds, because we love hearing them. They are the story of us.

When the turkey is presented, we ooh and ahh at the amazing culinary miracle that Mom pulls off every year. Cooking is one of Mom's love languages. And the bigger the turkey, the more the *love*.

As we share in the meal, partake of the good company, take turns doing the dishes or clearing the table, maybe even watch the holiday football game, there's an overarching knowing that this day is one of many that have come before and one of many that will come after. We're fully immersed in the *traditions* that give our family meaning and significance.

One thing we don't do is complain about the meal. We realize that we're not at a restaurant; we're not there to be waited on; we're not there to critique the food. In fact, it's the opposite. Everyone chips in, serving one another with glad hearts. We're grateful to be a part of this joyous gathering with people we love and who love us. So we form a circle, look one another in the eyes, hold hands, give thanks, and remember our good and great God.

It's my opinion that the holiday meal is a great metaphor for what we should endeavor to accomplish in our worship services each Sunday morning. Through our gathering, our stories, our shared traditions, our artistry, and our love for one another, we embody what it is to be the church in worship. These necessary elements actually have a deeper theology of worship that determines their importance, and an understanding of this theology will enrich our worship experience. While no metaphor is perfect, I think the holiday meal helps us paint a picture of what worship can be.

THE CHURCH IN COMMUNITY

We gather as God's family, everyone together—young and old, male and female, rich and not so rich, liberal and conservative, people of different racial and cultural backgrounds. We gather as an accepting, inclusive, grace-filled community. And more than just gather, we do the "one anothers"—we serve one another, care for one another, pray for and fellowship with and love one another. We understand that this thing we do is all about our relationships with one another based on our shared relationship with God. We're related by the blood of Christ, so no one is left out.

Consider Hebrew worship in the Old Testament. The covenant that God made with humankind was not strictly with individuals (such as Abraham) but was more fully realized with his people (the descendants of Abraham). The Hebrews had a different mindset than us westernized North Americans. We have a very individualized way of defining ourselves. We're fiercely independent, singular, unique, with rights and privileges and the pride of self-reliance. But the Hebrews saw themselves more so as small parts of a greater whole—God's chosen people. Each person was one link in the chain, one star in the constellation, one part of the people of God. This concept is later confirmed in the New Testament, where all believers are considered part of one body and the bride of Christ (see 1 Corinthians 12:12-30; Ephesians 5:25, 32; Revelation 21:9-10). Indeed, the first-century followers of the Way certainly acted as a people of God.

Just as in any healthy family, there's a profound joy that is created when all the members come together around a big dinner table. When we're together, we can understand ourselves more completely, enjoy our existence more fully, and better celebrate the story of what God has made in this family. One of my great joys in leading worship is when I see the congregation fully engaged and alive to the reality of God in the room. These are people I know personally, people I have laughed with, cried with, prayed for, lived life with. When I am up front and I look into the eyes of someone with arms raised and voice strong, that person leads me in worship. Their encouragement keeps me going so I can lead with continued passion. This experience is in stark contrast to some worship services where, in the midst of darkened auditoriums and concert-level sound, congregations are shrouded with anonymity and separateness.

This idea of the essential nature of community didn't originate with the church but comes from the essence of our trinitarian God, who is in his very being a community of love. There is only one God, but in the unity of the Godhead there are three eternal persons, the same in substance but distinct. God is the Father (John 6:25-59; Ephesians 4:6), the Son (Matthew 3:17; Hebrews 1), and the Spirit (John 14:26; Acts 2). The three persons of the Trinity are associated equally and as one (Matthew 28:19; 2 Corinthians 13:14). In other words, God exists in perfect community.

Each of the three persons has a unique identity. The Father is our Abba, our Daddy God. The Father sent his Son, and through the Son we become children of the Father. Jesus is our Savior, the perfect Lamb, who came to earth in flesh to die on the cross and be raised from the tomb on our behalf. Through him all things were made. Those who trust in Jesus make him our Lord, and we become his disciples. We cannot truly know God outside of the person of Jesus (Hebrews 1:1-2). Jesus left us the Holy Spirit, our Teacher, Guide, Comforter, and Power, and it is in cooperation with the Spirit that we are transformed.

The three persons of the Godhead exist in an ever-joyful, ever-creative community. Now here's the thing: worship is an invitation into community. In other words, God exists in perfect and eternal community, and through his grace he invites us, as a community of believers, into this Godhead community when we gather in worship. This is just how God designed us. We were made to be in community vertically with God and horizontally with one another. So there is this invitation and interaction, both vertical and horizontal, in corporate worship.

Our gathering then acknowledges two essential facts of our theology: one, that we enter into the presence of the community of the Godhead; and two, that we are at our core all members of God's redeemed community, bonded together by the love of God. We are no longer our own, but we surrender to Christ and belong to one another. Thus our gathering brings us definition, identity, and purpose.

Our family reflects who we are—including generational, gender, racial, and socioeconomic diversity. This isn't a politically correct diversity. It's a God-breathed diversity, an accepting, inclusive, grace-filled community. In this community there are young and old, men and women and children, people of color, and people of different cultural backgrounds. People of different economic backgrounds, temperaments, ideologies, and languages. And together, we're the church. Here we know and are known. That's who we are.[1]

TELLING GOD'S STORY

Another aspect of our metaphor of the holiday meal is that we tell God's story. When we gather for Thanksgiving or Christmas, we tell our stories to one another to catch up on what's happening. We share funny anecdotes, talk about people we know, even share inside jokes and things that define us. Our stories are a part of the larger story that is our family.

This story metaphor is also an aspect of our corporate worship. The story of all that was and is and is to come is the story of God. This larger story, sometimes referred to as the Christian metanarrative, is a crucial element in understanding our Christian faith, for it is the story of God's activity in the universe through time. A metanarrative can be defined as an overarching, comprehensive explanation that gives meaning to history, experience, and knowledge. It's like a narrative about narratives, a grand story that ties everything together. The Christian metanarrative of all that was and is and is to come can be described as the continuing three-act play of creation, fall, and redemption.

Dr. Robert Webber contends that "worship tells and acts out the story of God's saving work in history."[2] And if you look at the worship of the Bible, you'll see this is true. One of the primary ways the people of Israel worshiped was through many feasts and commemorations that tell the story of God's people, including Passover and Yom Kippur. Their worship is centered on retelling God's story. So worship is not only an encounter with God, it's also an encounter with the truth of God—not only who he is but also what he has done and continues to do.

In our corporate worship we remind one another of the things God has done for us, his mighty acts of power and grace, and how he came to become human, dwell among us, die on the cross, and be resurrected for our sake. We retell the story through Scripture readings, liturgies, prayers, sermons, and the most poetic of all sacred actions, the Lord's Supper. We retell the story of God through celebrations of Advent and Lent and Holy Week, from the manger to the cross to the sky. We tell these same ancient stories to one another every year, and it never gets old. Webber states, "Biblical remembering is much more than an intellectual recalling. Biblical remembering brings God's saving events to mind, body, and soul. . . . The word *remembrance* (in Greek, *anamnesis*) has the force of 'making present,' 'making alive,' 'making real.'"[3]

In the midst of this metanarrative is the crux of all time: Jesus Christ. Jesus—in the incarnation, crucifixion, and resurrection—is the primary character in the central event in all of history. So we respond to this metanarrative by inserting our smaller stories of how Jesus saved us into God's story, our lives enfolding into God's larger unfolding drama. We're reminded that God is the author of days, and we respond to this revelation in humility, gratitude, and obedience. We respond in worship. This is why sacramental actions, creeds, Scripture readings, Scripture-based songs, and an adherence to the historical church calendar remain important, especially in current times. The telling of the story of God through these elements helps to ground us to something deeper than ourselves.

Consider the rhythms of the Christian church calendar. Most evangelical churches have adopted a more superficial annual cycle focused on Mother's and Father's Days, Memorial Day, and the Fourth of July. While there's nothing wrong with celebrating these days, these are generally secular events manufactured by our culture. They don't necessarily help anchor us to our faith. For example, without the historical church calendar, Holy Week becomes Holy Day, and the story of Jesus—the garden, the table, the arrest, the trial, the cross, the entombment, and the resurrection—gets shoved into one Sunday. We lose sight of the deeper meanings of this and other events, and we lose the opportunity to respond in worship to them. In the process, we may have lost the greater sense of God's hand in history and how it applies to us today.

If one of our goals is to tell God's story, the church calendar helps us do this. In our worship we're invited into seasons of waiting, fasting, seeking, and preparing (such as the four Sundays of Advent and the forty days of Lent), specific days for reflecting on the drama of the cross (such as Holy Week), lengthy holidays of celebrating God's redemption through Christ's incarnation and resurrection (such as the twelve days of Christmastide and the fifty days of Eastertide), and days that remind us of God's empowering mission to bring others into his kingdom (such as Epiphany and Pentecost). God's story is told and celebrated in this ancient yearly cycle. Some evangelical churches are beginning to adopt greater portions of the church calendar because they understand that such practices create a greater corporate awareness of the story of God, particularly with the Advent story and the Easter story, the manger and the cross.

Within the context of the metanarrative, we invite others to tell their stories. People share their testimonies, prayer requests, and life events in the service, or through sacraments such as baptism. And as we do so, we remind ourselves how each of our smaller stories is a part of God's grand story, beautifully entwined through his bride, the church. We know and are known; we pray for one another; we bind our hearts together. And we remind one another that each of our stories is a part of the larger story of God's redemptive action in the universe.

SHARED TRADITIONS

In my family, Christmas has many silly traditions. For example, my father-in-law always gets chocolate-covered cherries. And nobody knows why. The kids always get new toothbrushes and gum in their stockings. We have an old felt calendar that we use to count down the twenty-five days of Christmas. My mother-in-law always makes a huge chocolate Texas sheet cake or bakes homemade pies. And the most important of all traditions: don't wake up Daddy, because he had a late night leading the Christmas Eve candlelight services.

Local churches have their traditions as well. Some churches have singing Christmas tree events, children's gift drives, or caroling around town. Some have a decorated tree or a living nativity scene or a candlelight Christmas Eve service, or some other aspect that's specific to their church. These traditions enrich us, giving meaning and identity to what we do and who we are.

The historical church has its own traditions as well, traditions that help ground us in our faith and connect us with the saints through history and around the world. Even the practice of meeting on Sunday mornings is a tradition passed down to us. Many of these common practices trace back to the first-century church, and others developed through our denominational traditions and even our local faith communities. There are ancient traditions such as singing the Doxology, lighting candles during Advent, and using palm fronds on Palm Sunday, and recent traditions such as worship choruses and video liturgies. Even the corporate personality and style of our local churches flow into the traditions we create. These traditions enrich us, form us, define us. They give us meaning and connect us to the greater community of believers past and present. While churches differ in approach, style, and methodology, we still share traditions that bind us together.

Let's consider one shared tradition that's the quintessential example of telling God's story: the Lord's Supper. When Jesus took the bread and the wine, he didn't start from scratch. He was celebrating the Passover meal with his disciples. This meal, celebrated from generation to generation, was already the commemoration of the most important event in the history of the nation Israel—when God saved them from captivity and brought them out of Egypt.

But Jesus had an even bigger story to tell. So he took the bread and the cup, already symbols of God's redemption, already a part of the tradition of the Jewish people, and recast them in a brand-new story of redemption. It was the foreshadowing act of the cross: the bread is his body; the wine is his blood. In a sense, he overlayed the story of the cross on the story of the exodus. And by implication, he connected them through the covenantal promise. It's an extraordinarily beautiful, artistic action.

Jesus told his disciples his story, and his *telling* became part of the overarching story. Then he commanded us to continue to tell and retell the story through all generations (1 Corinthians 11:23-26).

It doesn't matter much whether we share a chalice or drink from small plastic containers, or if we use unleavened bread or wafers. These are just a part of the shared traditions of our local or denominational affiliations. What does matter is that we not treat the tradition as a rote exercise, but instead derive meaning and significance from it. In the presence of the living Jesus at the table, we remember his love for us. And as we share the bread and the cup together, we also share the love poured out to us. When I think deeply about this, I'm overwhelmed by the poetry and transcendence that Jesus displayed for us. And every time we celebrate the Lord's Supper, we continue the tradition that goes back two thousand years.

When I was growing up, the word *tradition* had bad connotations. It suggested inflexibility, closed-mindedness, stuffy, old. But now in my more enlightened days, I understand that traditions can be good. They ground us. They help us derive meaning and significance. We should revel in the church traditions that have been handed down to us as well as the traditions we've created ourselves, because traditions are expressions of who we are.

EXPRESSIONS OF THE ARTS

The fourth aspect of our family meal metaphor is that we delight in the *artistry*. In our family, we make a big deal of decorating during Christmas. You know those designer trees that look perfect and everything matches, like they fell off a display at Pottery World? Yeah, well, our tree is the opposite. We have an assortment of eclectic ornaments, and some of them are chipped and scarred. None of them matches. But most of these ornaments have memories attached to them. Some of them go back to when our children were born, and even to my wife's childhood. Some of them were given to us by very dear friends. They're precious to us, meaningful and beautiful and personal and true.

The arts are an important expression in many churches, and rightly so. But often these expressions are simply a means to an end, a way to get more people through the doors, or a vehicle for a message. But there are inherent dangers in this approach. Francis Schaeffer warned that when "art is only an embodiment of a message . . . this view reduces art to an intellectual statement and the work of art as a work of art disappears."[4] This is why Christian music, Christian art, and Christian movies sometimes are second-rate. When churches see the arts as a vehicle for a message, they're always in danger of devolving their art into mere spectacle.

But there's another way. The arts should be considered an essential expression of kingdom life, for they allow us to express what can't be expressed with words. The arts also help us convey beauty, which is a type of truth that ultimately points to God the Creator. And, of course, the arts can be an expression of God's people in worship. So rather than use the arts (and the artists) as outreach tools, they should be unleashed to be an expression of who we are as God's children.[5]

This is a subtle but important difference. The arts in a church— music, dance, drama, visual arts, and many other art forms— should be an honest expression of the artists who are a part of the church. Artists of faith have a God-given role to share their gifts and talents within the body, to express truth and beauty in the church and in the world. This is the calling of Bezalel, and I believe it's the responsibility of the church to unleash artists of faith in this way. So the church's role shouldn't be to create spectacle, but to create opportunities for its many creatives to express their love for God in the artistic ways to which they're endowed and called. In this way, it isn't as much entertainment as it is engagement.

In my church are musicians who play drums, bass, and electric guitar, but also musicians who play less popular instruments like the trombone, cello, and mandolin. Writers compose liturgies. Painters and sculptors display in our art gallery. Actors act and write sketches and scripts. Technical artists mix sound and set lighting. Dancers dance during an offertory or call to worship. Creatives are given the opportunity to express themselves and their stories through their art to the community of believers in which they belong.

It's like the difference between a Pottery World Christmas tree, shiny and new and perfectly matching but impersonal, and the family Christmas tree, imperfect and not matching but full of meaningful and personal expressions of beauty. As God's children, our artistic expressions can put a smile on God's face in the same way that our children's crayon art delights us.

ALL YOU NEED IS LOVE

The fifth and final aspect in our metaphor is that we gather to express our love and thankfulness to God. A number of years ago, our family was invited to Thanksgiving by friends who had no faith background. These friends were generous and maybe had a few perfectionist tendencies, and when we came over, there was a perfect golden turkey, a perfect table, perfect place settings, and all the fixings, which of course were also perfect. After some friendly banter and the usual chaos associated with setting several families down at the table, we had a sudden moment when a quiet settled on us, everyone eyeing the bountiful spread before us. Then our hostess announced gleefully, "Okay, let's eat!" And we all dug in.

But we never prayed. On Thanksgiving Day, we never actually gave thanks.

Later, after we got home and the kids were in bed, I mulled over that a while. In our worship services, we can go through the motions of worship—singing, standing, praying, and listening to the sermon—but never telling Jesus we love him, we appreciate him, we thank him, we adore him. If we aren't purposeful in our worship, we can become "a resounding gong or a clanging cymbal" (1 Corinthians 13:1).

Above all things, our corporate worship should be characterized by a love for God and a love for one another. Remember that one of the elements of first-century worship was the agape feast. Also called the love feast, the agape feast was a communal meal shared among followers of the Way and was often attached to the Eucharist meal, the Lord's Supper (*Eucharist* comes from the Greek *eucharistos*, which means "grateful" or "thankful"). In a way, every Sunday worship service should have a sense of agape permeating our actions and attitudes, our fellowship and worship.

FAMILY MEAL OR THEME RESTAURANT

The family meal relates to several elements of healthy corporate worship. However, church attenders often see the worship service through the lenses of another metaphor: the theme restaurant.

Theme restaurants are highly stylized, efficiently run, high in quality, corporate, and cookie cutter. There's a lot of memorabilia on the walls, a lot of wow in the room, a lot of flair pinned to the suspenders of the servers. They're fun to visit, and the food can be pretty good. But there's no feeling of being with family, no sense of tradition or shared story, no invitation to enter into something meaningful. Ultimately there's nothing in a theme restaurant that is *honest*. Style overtakes substance, friendliness replaces friendship, love is supplanted by experiential satisfaction.

Too many times, we as worshipers fall into the trap of wanting to be catered to instead of truly being a part. We become enamored with the flair and resist the inherent messiness of fellowship. We want the theme restaurant because there we get a fancy meal without having to do any cooking.

But worship is intended to be something we bring ourselves to and participate in, not something done to us or for us. We bring ourselves into the presence of God. We bring our stories of redemption and enfold them into the larger story of God. We bring ourselves into imperfect and wonderful relationships with the people of God. We enter into the eternal dialogue. And the church demands more than just attendance. The church is, in the best way possible, an opportunity to lose ourselves in the greater identity of the bride communing with the groom.

Again, liturgies are all around us, and they shape us in good and bad ways. Just as there is a type of liturgy to the family traditions that make up our holiday meals, so there is a liturgy to the worship service, and this forms our souls. When the church gathers, there is more going on than we know.

WORSHIP PRACTICE

A metanarrative is like a tapestry that God is weaving, and we're all threads in this tapestry. While our life thread has a beginning and an end, it's nevertheless entwined into God's eternal patterns of redemptive action in the universe, interacting with many other threads through time. In a way, your threads can be traced back through the person who first told you about God's grace and the person who told him or her, through the Reformers, through the saints and missionaries, through the first-century martyrs, through Paul, Peter, and the disciples, and all the way to Christ on the cross. These threads form patterns on the tapestry, one of God's perfect design. It's an amazing thought to ponder.

If you're in a small group, take the time to tell your stories of faith to one another. In this way, you share your small but significant parts of the metanarrative. Our stories give us meaning and help bind us together. As you testify, bear in mind that you are part of the tapestry that God is weaving through history and humanity.

Eight

THE RHYTHM OF WORSHIP

Remember the Sabbath day by keeping it holy.

EXODUS 20:8

WHEN I WAS A LITTLE KID, one of the hardest things for me to do was take a nap. I have vague recollections of my mom coaxing me onto the bed, telling me it was time to lie down, close my eyes, rest my head, and sleep. I also remember staring at the ceiling, bouncing my feet impatiently, watching time pass like molasses, as if minutes were years. Now in my adult years naps seem like luxury vacations that I can't afford, little oases of time in a vast desert of to-do lists and swelling email inboxes. There are moments when I stop in the middle of a fast-paced day and long for a nap. And I don't think I'm alone here.

Possibly the most neglected of the Ten Commandments is the command to remember the Sabbath and keep it holy. We cram as much activity into seven days as possible, and Sunday has become a whirlwind of kids' soccer matches, social events, football watching, and catching up on work. We resist the temptation to be still and devote "unproductive" time to our spiritual lives. But here's the thing: our souls require spiritual filling. Our souls—heart and mind and body—need rest.

In the midst of increasing secularism, perhaps we have lost a sense of the rhythm of worship, a rhythm that God has given to us and placed inside of us, both physiologically and spiritually. Perhaps rediscovering what it is to be a worshiper—and recapturing a worship culture in general—requires an embrace of the ancient practice of the Sabbath. Perhaps our deep yearning for rest and God's invitation to meet him in Sabbath are more than related—they were intended by him.

REDISCOVERING THE SABBATH

The concept of the Sabbath comes originally from the book of Genesis. God poetically spoke the world into existence in six days, and he rested on the seventh day. This concept is later fleshed out in God's commandment to "Remember the Sabbath day by keeping it holy. . . . For in six days the LORD made the heavens and the earth, the sea, and all that is in them, but he rested on the seventh day. Therefore the LORD blessed the Sabbath day and made it holy" (Exodus 20:8, 11).

The Hebrew tradition was to practice the Sabbath, a weekly day of abstinence from work intended to focus on themselves, one another, and especially God. The observance of the Sabbath was an important part of following God that reminded Israel of God's mighty power and acts of providence and also that they were to set aside time to worship him. Today sabbaticals are often granted by corporations, universities, and religious organizations, and last from a few weeks to a year. All this comes from the Hebrew concept of Sabbath.

Although God commanded the Sabbath, Jesus himself reminds us that the Sabbath shouldn't be simply a religious observance. In the book of Mark, Pharisees criticized some of Jesus' disciples for picking some heads of grain on the Sabbath day. But Jesus corrected the Pharisees regarding the intent of the Sabbath, not the rules of the Sabbath. "The Sabbath was made for man, not man for the Sabbath. So the Son of Man is Lord even of the Sabbath" (Mark 2:27-28). In other words, God commanded the Sabbath on our behalf. It was a gift to his people, not a rigid set of rules or a rigid ceremonial observance.

Traditionally the Hebrew Sabbath is Saturday. But because Jesus was raised on the day after the Sabbath, on Sunday, the first-century Christians began meeting on Sundays to honor the resurrection. The book of Acts says, "On the first day of the week we came together to break bread" (Acts 20:7). Over time, and as the Christian sect began to distance itself from the Jewish religion, Sunday became the primary day of observing the Sabbath. So every Sunday is, in a very real sense, like a little Easter. Every Sunday we celebrate that "Christ is risen. Christ is risen indeed."

The day of the week itself isn't as important as the concept. In other words, the letter of the law isn't as important as the spirit of the law, which is to take a day to rest the soul and focus on God (Romans 14:5; Colossians 2:16-17). So whether it is Sunday or Saturday or any day in between, God's intent is that we accept his invitation to rest in him. This resting has three aspects: we are to set aside a day in our week for rest, we are to take that day to gather as the people of God, and we are to be purposeful in making it holy and centered on God. In other words, there's a rhythm to rest, a rhythm to gathering, and a rhythm to worship.

PLAYING THE RESTS

From fourth grade all the way through college, I played clarinet in symphonic and marching and even Dixieland bands. This reveals one thing about me: I relate less to Spongebob and more to Squidward than I would like to admit. In any event, when I was in seventh-grade band, I was excited because our band director had just handed out the sheet music to a popular song called "Oye Como Va."

"Oye Como Va" was a groundbreaking song for its time, written by Tito Puente but popularized by the iconic Carlos Santana. In the midst of the musically evolving seventies, Santana introduced "Oye Como Va" and with it an entirely new genre of rock. Although it's a rock song, it has a Latin syncopation—what musicians call a groove or a pocket—that's deceptively difficult to play.

Now picture this: fifty or so pubescent boys and girls playing hard-grooving Latin rock with clarinets, trombones, flutes, and trumpets. The thought should make you shudder in horror. Our hapless band director would count out the tempo, and the entire band—driven by the adrenal glands of the drum section—would launch into the song about three times faster, five times louder, and a hundred times sloppier.

There was simply no way to stop the acceleration when we tried to play that song. It was like jumping out of an airplane; at the downbeat, gravity simply took over, and we did a free fall head first into terminal velocity. As we played the song faster and faster, our band director would become more frustrated, more irritated, more red in the face. Finally, in unmitigated exasperation, he hurled down his baton, rattled his music stand angrily, and stormed out of the band room. We all sat there, looking at each other.

One of the concepts music students naturally have a hard time with is the rest. A musical rest is an interval of silence with a specific duration that can last a single beat or less to several or more measures. Unless the musicians know how to "play" the rests, a song will implode into cacophony; music becomes noise. Music is defined as much by what notes you don't play as by what you do play, and by when you do or don't play them.

Unless a musician knows how to play the rests, a song will become a confused clamor, like downtown traffic. But I'm not actually referring to music—music is a metaphor for life. In the music of our lives, there are notes to play, but it's important to play the rests too. If we don't, our lives can quickly become noise. And though we think of rest as a lack of activity, that's not entirely true—especially as it relates to Sabbath and worship. As a musician, playing the rests is an active, mindful, purposeful act.

The controversial twentieth-century avant-garde composer John Cage once wrote a composition called "4'33," in which the orchestra deliberately played four minutes and thirty-three seconds of silence. The soloist and the entire orchestra sat quietly for that time, actively not playing. That was the entire piece. Cage had a point to make. His intention was not only to perform the silence but also to force the audience to listen to the background noise of the environment in which they sat. He wanted the audience to listen actively and engage in the silence.

There may be a lesson here. We are hardwired by God to both work and rest in regular intervals—physically, emotionally, spiritually. We aren't unlike music in this way. But I think we've become conditioned by our culture to the point that rest and silence have become uncomfortable to us. We've accepted stress and anxiety as a way of life. We've become numb to the noise and distractions and inner voices. Some of us desperately need to experience silence. We're starved for rest. We're starved for Sabbath.

As a simple matter of spiritual formation, we should embrace regular times of rest—daily, weekly, yearly. The Sabbath is a weekly cycle of rest, and I believe there's a genius to the regularity of it, a cycle that seems to match the human cycle. Our bodies need time to recharge and rejuvenate. There's a circadian rhythm designed right into us that's both physical and spiritual. The commandment to keep the Sabbath holy is for us as much as it is for God (Mark 2:27). That the Sabbath was modeled from the seven days of creation implies it's a part of the rhythm of the created order. God also ordains that rhythm to us and for us.

The word *rest* has implications that aren't just physical but emotional and spiritual as well. Rest your body. Rest your mind. Rest your soul. Rest in him. In a perfect world, we would schedule times of rest into the cycles of every day, every week, and every year.

THE RHYTHM OF GATHERING

One of the unfortunate consequences of our increasingly postmodern society is the trend toward unchurched Christians. These are people who profess a belief in Jesus Christ but don't attend a church or organized faith gathering. Barna Group's "The State of the Church 2016" states that while 73 percent of Americans self-identify as Christian, further polling reveals that only 31 percent are "practicing Christians," defined as a person who "attends a religious service at least once a month and says their faith is very important in their life."[1] This is in contrast to "The State of the Church 2011," which stated that roughly four in five self-identified as Christian, and 47 percent said they attended a church. This older report was quick to point out that "attendance at a church service in a given week has declined among self-identified Christians by nine percentage points since 1991."[2] For those who don't want to do the math, that's a drop of 16 percent in the last five years and 25 percent in the last twenty-five years. Clearly there's a marked decline in church attendance in general and specifically in the attendance of those who profess to be Christians.

There may be many reasons for this growing population of unchurched Christians: an increasing secularization of our culture, an increasing distrust of organized religion, an increasing belief in the privatization of faith, and the many issues I discuss in this book. Regardless of the reasons, we can point to some casualties. For one, I think many are starving themselves spiritually by foregoing regular worship experiences. But perhaps the greatest loss is of an understanding of what it is to truly be the bride of Christ, to be a part of a deeply rooted community of faith.

To illustrate this, I'd like to discuss the concept of incarnation. We understand what incarnation means as it relates to salvation. Jesus, in order to rescue us from our sins and invite us into his kingdom, incarnated or "became flesh." He inserted himself in bodily form into the universe to commune with us, to care for us, to teach us, and to sacrifice himself for us. In a very true sense, he is love incarnate. He is God's love that put on flesh. (As an aside, this is why the victory is as much present in the manger as it is on the cross, and why the celebration of Advent should be as important and as profound as Easter.)

We apply the concept of incarnation to ourselves as well. If we are to be Jesus to the world—to care for the widows and orphans, to minister to the poor, and to live out our faith—we must also incarnate God's love to the world. Thus, we are to "flesh out" God's love to others. As the body of Christ, we are God's hands and feet to the world. And so incarnation includes fleshing out God's love and purposes among those around us.

Now, have you ever considered the concept of incarnation as it relates to worship? How does one incarnate worship? Sabbath involves the idea of gathering together as God's people to give our attentions to our God. Leviticus says, "There are six days when you may work, but the seventh day is a day of sabbath rest, a day of sacred assembly" (23:3). So to incarnate our worship is to be present "in the flesh" with one another as we gather before God. Worship is a communal act, a shared act, an act that's horizontal as well as vertical. We gather as brothers and sisters in Christ, the priesthood of believers, the sacred assembly, where "there is neither Jew nor Gentile, neither slave nor free, nor is there male and female, for you are all one in Christ Jesus" (Galatians 3:28).

Sunday morning is one of the best parts of my week. We gather as a congregation with the shared experiences of having lived life together. In this community, we've laughed together, cried together, broken bread together, prayed for one another, shared life together. This is the imperfectly perfect beauty of the bride, a flesh-and-blood community of believers in Jesus. When we stand together, our presence is a testimony to our belief in the kingship of Jesus. We demonstrate faith, hope, love, and conviction with our presence.

When we stand before one another as the people of God, and I look in their eyes as they look in mine, we declare to one another, "Our God is true. Our God is good. Our God is real. Our God reigns in me." When I see people raise their arms and give themselves to worship, they remind me and others of the goodness and truth of God. Through our very presence, we encourage one another in worship. We have become an incarnation of God's love as a community of faith.

This is the sacred assembly, the church gathered, the church incarnated. Each of us comes with our stories of redemption. Our stories entwine when we gather, and they enfold into the larger story of God. Our gathering gives us meaning and identity that are greater and deeper than our individual selves. But you can't incarnate if you aren't in the room. You can't participate in community if you don't show up. You can't incarnate congregational worship if you aren't there in the flesh. Not only do you miss out on the essential act of communal worship, but those who are present lose the benefit of fullness of worship with you.

There is a sweetness to the sacred assembly that I often feel during times of worship, those moments when we are together and are more than just a crowd in a room. We are gathered in God's name, at his throne, for his glory. We are his people, his bride, his beloved. In those moments, among God's people and singing God's praises, I believe we are more ourselves than we know.

You see, the worship of our gathering does something to us. It fills us, encourages us, sustains us, binds our hearts together, and ultimately changes us. For worship is corporate spiritual formation. It is in the gathering of the people of God, in the presence of God the Father, through the kingship of Jesus and the prompting of the Holy Spirit. And when we gather to worship the one who should rightfully be worshiped, something becomes right with the world, something becomes right with our souls. So weekly worship becomes a formative practice that frames our lives and forms our souls. As James K. A. Smith asserts, "Worship is formative, not merely expressive."[3]

Ask any guitarist to play a song, and the first thing she'll do is check the tuning. She understands that it's normal for a guitar to float out of tune due to a variety of issues—temperature, humidity, loosened pegs, overuse, or underuse. All guitars need to be tuned regularly and often. And so it is with us. Regular and weekly worship helps us to retune, to set the strings of our soul back in sympathetic resonance with the Holy Spirit. Worship helps to remind us of what is right and true, and who is righteous and holy. And true worship is an act of humility and surrender, where we once again hand control of our lives over to God.

Weekly worship reminds us to live humbly and seek the kingdom. It encourages us to persevere in times of trial, uncertainty, and suffering, and to be sustained in times of sin and sorrow. We're reminded of the greater reality of who God is, what he has done, and what he has promised to do. Weekly worship helps fill the holes in our hearts with God.

We are sustained not only by grace directly from God but also by his grace through his people. When we worship together, our presence is a testimony to one another of the goodness of God. We look one another in the eye, and through a simple glance, we affirm to one another the goodness of God. Simply through our presence in the room, we push against the forces of darkness with the light of the greater truth—that God has already won the victory. Our God is greater, our God is stronger, our God is higher than any other.

EMBRACING THE RHYTHMS

As I stated at the beginning of the chapter, there's a rhythm to rest, a rhythm to gathering, and a rhythm to worship that is not only given to us, both as a command and as a gift, but also imbedded in us in physical and spiritual ways. For us to better live out the fullness of worship, we need to practice making Sunday worship a priority again. We need to reorient ourselves in such a way that our worship life flows out of the Sunday gathering—in our practices and actions, in our beliefs and attitudes, and in our personal and corporate worship.

What does the practice of the Sabbath look like practically? It begins first with planning the rest of your week in such a way that Sunday isn't filled with things to do and places to go. It includes a deliberate slowing throughout the day, a mindfulness of God in the moments of that day, a premeditated purposefulness toward making the day holy. There's an awareness that God will fill you up physically, emotionally, and spiritually.

This may include private prayer, devotional reading, and quiet time in preparation for meeting God in corporate worship. It does include gathering with a community of faith to fellowship and to worship. The Sunday worship service becomes the high point of the worship life, where we approach the sacred ground and meet our holy God together. As in ancient times, this gathering is marked by an attitude of agape, God's love permeating through us to others and back to him. As in all spiritual disciplines, the practice of the Sabbath is consistently repeated. As in all spiritual disciplines, in the repetition—in the rhythm—our souls are formed.

I mentioned earlier the Santana tune "Oye Como Va." Many people know the song, yet few people know what the title means. Interestingly, it has two different meanings. Said alone, it can mean, "Hey, how's it going?" But along with the musical response *"mi ritmo,"* it also means, "Listen to how my rhythm goes" (*Oye como va mi ritmo*).

I think God gave us the Sabbath because he has a rhythm, and he invites us into it. There's a rhythm to rest because our hearts, minds, bodies, and souls need rest. There's a rhythm to gathering, because we need one another; we need the fellowship of the church. And there's a rhythm to worship, because we need God. God gives us the Sabbath for all these reasons, and in constancy, faithfulness, and rhythm we can best live the life of worship God intends for us. We need to take the time to listen to God's rhythm, to how God's rhythm goes.

May we all learn how to live in the rhythms of God's grace.

WORSHIP PRACTICE

Take a Sabbath as the practice for this chapter. Start on the weekdays, preparing yourself for the upcoming Sunday by clearing your schedule, running your errands, doing what you need to do to make Sunday a stress-free and less active day. On Saturday night, go to bed earlier. On Sunday, practice the art of slowing—physically, emotionally, spiritually. Mentally and spiritually prepare for the shared experience of corporate worship. Go to church early and stay late. Continue the practice of slowing through the remainder of the Sunday. If you have a family, participate in a family-oriented, low-tech event (like a board game or jigsaw puzzle). Have a family meal, but don't make it a big production. Eat together at the dinner table. And in all your activities of the day, be mindful of God's presence and thankful for his blessings.

Nine

EVERYDAY EXPRESSIONS OF WORSHIP

Sing to the LORD, praise his name;
proclaim his salvation day after day.

PSALM 96:2

ONE OF OUR FAMILY TRADITIONS is Mother's Day, and it's pretty much the same every year. I buy a pretty bouquet of flowers for Debbie the day before. The girls often create a special breakfast for Mom that morning, accompanied by a handmade Mother's Day card. Our sons make a valiant attempt at cleaning the kitchen. Even the cats behave that day. I end up cooking some semblance of a dinner (or just buying takeout). And we do this because we want Mom to feel extra-special on that extra-special day.

But on Monday, everything goes back to normal. The kids go back to the routine of getting ready for school, packing lunches, and rushing out the door. I sleep in after a long day of church. And Debbie goes back to cleaning the kitchen, making the meals, paying the bills, running the house. Even the cats revert to their aloof indifference. The bouquet sits quietly on the kitchen counter, a slowly wilting memory of Mom's special day.

That's the way we are with God sometimes. Sunday is God's day, and we go out of our way to meet with him. We attend the church service, gather as his people, sing his praises, read our Bibles, and honestly crave the presence of God. But then Monday comes, and we generally ignore him.

Is God as real to us on Monday as he is on Sunday? When we gather, we really do believe that the God of the universe— the God who made the galaxies and the stars and the mountains and the seas—communes with us on Sunday morning. He invades the small spaces of our sanctuaries, pervades our worship, stirs our hearts. And we are intent and purposeful to try to hear his still, small voice. But what happens the other six days of the week?

In his book *Unceasing Worship*, Harold Best presents a compelling definition of worship: "Worship is the continuous outpouring of all that I am, all that I do and all that I can ever become in light of a chosen or choosing [God]."[1] This definition is packed with meaning, but what strikes me is the term "continuous outpouring." And it's true. Worship is an eternal event, happening through history, through creation, and in the heavens and the earth. Worship is a relentless and lavish pouring out of ourselves in response to a God who is relentlessly holy and loving and worthy. Truly it should be normative for Christ followers that our worship be unceasing, pouring like a river into the entirety of our lives.

So, is God as real to you on Monday as he is on Sunday? If so, what does honest worship look like the other six days of the week? How do we manifest worship that is unceasing throughout the week and throughout our lives?

EXPRESSIONS OF LOVE

In his book *The Five Love Languages*, Gary Chapman introduced the concept that people can express and receive love in specific ways and that each person gives and receives these languages differently. While the theory may appear simplistic, I've found it to have very helpful practical application in our family. For example, one of my wife's primary love languages is acts of service. And one of my primary love languages is food. So when Debbie cooks a big meal for me, I feel loved by her. Likewise, when I clean the kitchen afterward—knowing she hates to clean the kitchen—she feels loved by me. When we were first married, we knew this about one another, so we made a deal. She does the cooking, and I do the cleaning. This is one of the ways we learned to show love to one another in the ordinary moments and rhythms of our day.

As my children have matured, we've come to know their love languages as well. One enjoys receiving gifts. One appreciates quality time. They all appreciate physical touch as a practical demonstration of love. Knowing what love language to "speak into" each of our children and into one another has helped us stay in tune in our relationships. Knowing turns into practices, practices become habits, and habits become a lifestyle. This has helped us form a strong marriage and strong family ties.

This raises a deeper and perhaps peculiar question: Does God have love languages? In other words, are there ways God prefers us to demonstrate our love to him? Can knowing God's love languages help us make worship a lifestyle? Although we can rightfully assert that "God is love" (1 John 4:8), God *expresses* his love to us through a variety of means: his Word, his blessings, his mighty acts, and his Son. We respond by expressing our love back to him, creating demonstrations of worship. This vertical love conversation begins and ends with God (1 John 4:19). It's my opinion that understanding what pleases God and making those practices a regular part of our lives help us strengthen our relationship with him and help us stay in tune with him. So how do we express love to God in a way he wishes to receive it?

To answer this question, let's first remind ourselves of the nature of the relationship into which we're invited. Jesus reminds us at the beginning of the Lord's Prayer that our relationship is kingly but also paternal (Matthew 6:9)—for we worship Abba Father, Daddy God. His relationship with us is both holy and intimate. We kneel before the throne, but we're also invited to sit on his lap. "See what great love the Father has lavished on us, that we should be called children of God! And that is what we are!" (1 John 3:1). So I encourage you to keep this Abba relationship in mind as we explore God's love languages.

For the sake of discussion, I've identified five elements that the Bible indicates as love languages for God: presence, obedience, faith, loving others, and work. Perhaps you can come up with some as well.

Presence. God invites us into a dynamic and ongoing relationship with him. From Adam's encounter with God in the garden in Genesis 3, to Paul's startling encounter with Jesus on the road to Damascus in Acts 9, to the Holy Spirit's calling to us today, God has sought a restored and ongoing relationship with humanity. This relationship is not a static, distant one; God is intimate and involved, caring and nurturing, active and alive.

We're invited to come near to God, as he comes near to us (James 4:8). We can come with our deepest and rawest thoughts and emotions, as the book of Psalms teaches us. And Jesus himself modeled this intimate relationship through the practices of prayer and solitary time with his Father God (see, for example, Mark 1:35; Luke 5:16; 22:39-44). So giving God our time and attention—we might say our *presence*—can be considered a love language that speaks to our desire for intimacy with him, and him with us. For our God is an ever-present God, and he desires that we be present with him.

There are two main categories of ways to be present with God. The first involves specific and structured time. Examples of such disciplines include having morning or evening devotions, practicing the divine office, and having specific weekend or weeklong retreats to focus on God. These moments can include prayer, meditation, journaling, Bible study, singing and listening to sacred music, or reading Christian books. Those of us who are more creative may use our commute time, or take a slow walk or bike ride in the evening, or have a prayer closet or space in which to be with God. The point is to have specific and concentrated time with him regularly.

The second means of presence is to foster an awareness of God throughout the day. The seventeenth-century monk Nicholas Herman of Lorraine, better known as Brother Lawrence, is well-known for delineating a way to practice and cultivate a constant awareness of God.[2] Even in the mundane actions of peeling potatoes or washing dishes, Lawrence encourages us to have an awareness of God's presence and to worship and interact with him in the ordinariness of life.

To practice the presence, some people play Christian music through the day, place reminder prayer cards on their bathroom mirror or computer screen, or use short centering prayers throughout the day. Some even fast. I've put on a prayer bracelet during the season of Lent as a trigger to keep me God-centric. While 24/7 awareness of God may be unattainable for ordinary mortals like me, the point is to foster a continuing conversation with God, a God-awake attitude hour to hour, moment to moment.

Obedience. One of the very simple ways my children please me is by doing what I ask of them. When they were little, it was eating their vegetables, picking up their LEGOs, and playing nice with their siblings. As they matured, obedience had more to do with driving the car in a safe manner, doing their chores, and honoring their curfews. When our children respond to our rules and requests with willingness and submission, they demonstrate respect and alignment to us as parents, and we respond with pride and satisfaction. We also understand that their obedience isn't mere rule following but is from a heart that increasingly reflects our habits, values, and convictions.

Jesus explained that we are branches attached to the vine, and we're intended to produce good fruit by remaining attached. He said, "If you keep my commands, you will remain in my love, just as I have kept my Father's commands and remain in his love" (John 15:10). To remain—or abide, as some versions state it—is to follow or to act in accordance with. To be clear, Jesus wasn't implying that the love of God is conditional. He was saying that his obedience to his heavenly Father was an act of love, and that we should do the same. This should make sense. We can't expect to have a full and intimate relationship with God if our hearts are in contention with him. Neither can we worship as intended (Psalm 24:3-4).

It's also clear in John 15 that God expects us to be fruitful. Just as we expect our obedient children to prosper and thrive as they grow in character, so God expects us to bear fruit through our continuing discipleship. Jesus declared, "This is to my Father's glory, that you bear much fruit, showing yourselves to be my disciples" (John 15:8). So God is pleased by our obedience, an obedience that bears the fruit of "love, joy, peace, forbearance, kindness, goodness, faithfulness, gentleness and self-control" (Galatians 5:22-23). In this way, our Father may consider obedience, or abiding in his will, a love language.

Faith. Related to obedience is faith. "Faith is confidence in what we hope for and assurance about what we do not see" (Hebrews 11:1). The book of Hebrews eloquently describes how the ancients—Abel, Enoch, Noah, Abraham, Sarah, Moses, and others—gave their lives to the promises of God, proving their loyalty and conviction to the vision that God had given to them. Where obedience can be seen as the consistent abiding in the will of God—that is, keeping his commands—faith is a trust or confidence in God and in his promises.

God highly values faith. Faith is the requisite for salvation, for the saving grace that changes our story from one of darkness to light. As we read in Ephesians, "For it is by grace you have been saved, through faith—and this is not from yourselves, it is the gift of God—not by works, so that no one can boast" (Ephesians 2:8-9). But faith is more than just a one-time decision. Faith requires a continual future focus, a firm belief that God won't forsake us in times of trial but will carry us to completion in whatever purposes he has for us. In a sense, faith is the engine that propels us through the story of redemption that the Author of Days is writing in the universe.

Abraham's faith in the promises of God allowed him to participate in the story as the father of a great nation. Moses' faith allowed him to participate in the story as the one who led his people out of bondage and to the threshold of the Promised Land. David's faith allowed him to slay the giant, defeat armies, and build a great nation. We're all a part of this redemptive metanarrative. Faith is believing that God has a plan for each of us, and he will carry it to completion.

Finally, faith pleases God, and without faith, it's impossible to please him (Hebrews 11:6). So demonstrations of faith can be a love language to God. We can't worship without faith, and our demonstrations of faith, both large and small, are a way we worship throughout the week. At the end of our days, our highest aspiration is that God would affirm us with "Well done, good and faithful servant!" (Matthew 25:21).

Loving others. Jesus was clear, in word and deed, that our love of God should extend to a love for others. In his parable of the sheep and goats, he offered both an encouragement and a warning: "Whatever you did for one of the least of these brothers and sisters of mine, you did for me" (Matthew 25:40). As his people, we are his expression of love to the world. In fact, God intends to save the world through the church, for we are his hands and feet—his boots on the ground—to love others in tangible ways.

As noted previously, the commandment to love the Lord with heart, soul, mind, and strength is central to worship. And Jesus added a second command: "Love your neighbor as yourself" (Matthew 22:39). Essentially he tethers the Golden Rule to the great commandment. We'll dwell on this subject more deeply later, but for now let's simply note that loving others can be considered one of God's love languages, given that Jesus said our actions toward others are actions toward him (Matthew 25:35-36).

Work. Work may seem an odd addition to this list. For most people, work is a curse, something we endure between weekends and vacations. But God's plan for us seems more expansive. In the Garden of Eden God first invited Adam to work under and with him in his plan for creation (Genesis 2:15), and throughout the Bible, we see God providing the means for humankind to flourish and prosper.

Let's back up and take a side street for a moment. The first five words of the Bible describe God as an eternally creative being: "In the beginning God created" (Genesis 1:1). Thus our creative ability is a vital aspect of being made in the image of God. Further, creativity and workmanship are necessary components to fulfill the cultural mandate, God's job description for humanity: "be fruitful and increase in number; fill the earth and subdue it" (Genesis 1:28). This includes the blessing to prosper and pro-create, to care for and steward the earth, and to create and to express ourselves in the universe. Our need to create, organize, and thrive is imbedded in our DNA, and it's mandated as a part of our purpose here on earth. Work, then, is a crucial aspect of crafting and sustaining culture, and God intends us to work as part of our creative calling. In a very real sense, we're called to come alongside God's creative glory and incorporate our work-manship with his.

Have you ever taken a child's crayon drawing and hung it on your refrigerator door? Maybe it was a drawing of a kitty or a race car or a colorful doodle with a yellow sun in the corner. Why did you do that? Because the art was good? Perhaps, but you probably hung it because you loved the child. And that artwork represented a part of who that child is. That creation was a heartfelt expression of someone you love. Well, this is how God feels about us. Every creative and culture-making expression done for the King delights the King. For he delights in our prospering, our flourishing, our working with all our might for his glory.

Crafting culture is more than painting a painting or composing a song. Culture making is a plumber installing a water heater, a chef creating a meal, a football coach drawing up a new play, a man stacking wood. Culture making is done by architects and engineers, athletes and farmers, comedians and pastry chefs, scientists modeling the double helix, and stay-at-home parents reading bedtime stories. The ability to craft culture is a quality shared by all of humanity.

And God is glorified when we craft culture, when we skillfully and responsibly create, produce, and labor for his glory. Dorothy Sayers famously declared, "The only Christian work is good work well done."[3] So work—whether vocation or hobby—can be a love language to God when done with excellence and spiritual purpose.

But Christians generally have an underdeveloped theology of work. The office or job site is seen as secular, far from the churchy or spiritual things that are ascribed to Sundays. Thus we live dichotomous lives, sacred in one place and secular in the other places. Unfortunately our actions and attitudes in the other places become secular as well.

Perhaps we need a deeper theology, one that sees our places of work as sacred: our desks as altars and our coworkers as people God loves. Then we can see that our actions and attitudes, and the very quality of our work, matter. For God is with us in our boardrooms, jobsites, and workstations, and he invites us to redeem our time, our actions, and our relationships in them. So our work—the quality of it and the attitude that begets it—is a testimony to others and a means of glorifying God.

Johann Sebastian Bach famously ascribed the initials "S.D.G." on many of his works, an abbreviation for the Latin term *soli Deo gloria*, "to God alone be the glory." It was his way of proclaiming that the musical piece was intended to glorify God and not himself or anything else. Whether it was a sacred cantata performed in the church or a simple two-part invention composed to instruct harpsichord students in the parlor, his intention was to glorify God through every work.

YOUR MILEAGE MAY VARY

A few caveats may be in order. First, although Chapman limits his love languages to five, there may be many others, depending on how you define them. What I've presented isn't an exhaustive list but a rudimentary attempt to provide a different spin on some of the spiritual disciplines. What's most important is the concept of love languages and how it can help us express our love back to God in ways we can actually express them and in ways that he will receive them. So feel free to come up with your own love languages to God, ones that are meaningful to you and glorifying to God.

Second, we must keep in mind the consequential issue of being and not just doing. We aren't just going through the motions

Monday through Saturday. If we're truly approaching God with humility and submission, he will use love languages to transform us into worshipers in greater and greater ways. Our presence before God—in silence, solitude, meditation, journaling—can be a catalyst to uncover our true self. Purposeful obedience to God's law can help root out the justifications for our secret sins. Serving others in a soup kitchen can reframe our perspectives and give us a spirit of gratitude. And our creative works can not only glorify God but also feed our souls. This is the dynamic of the God conversation: the revelation and response of the spiritual language not only glorifies God, it also changes us in the process.

Third, we're called into an Abba relationship, for we are children of God. Childhood isn't a perfect process. There are skinned knees and boo-boos to kiss, selfish "mine!" moments, and a thousand imperfections. Not one of us will live perfectly intentioned, disciplined, faultless lives. Thankfully, God grants us grace in our imperfect attempts at giving him our hearts in worship each day of the week.

LIVING HALLELUJAH

Hallelujah is a common Hebrew phrase in the Bible that translates to "Praise to you, Jehovah" or "Praise you, Lord." Indeed, no less than ten worship psalms begin with this phrase. It's also the most common Hebrew phrase used in modern worship lyrics; as a leader and songwriter, I've both sung and written *hallelujah* many times. In other words, the Hebrew word has become a part of the English language.

A number of years ago, during a songwriting session, I decided to add a twist to this somewhat tired lyrical trope by writing a chorus that begins, "We are your hallelujah." It's not enough just to sing the word. We, as God's people, need to embody the word. We need to live out that phrase, so that our lives became an expression of glory. We need to *be* the hallelujah that praises God.

As we continue to learn how to speak God's love languages in our own individual ways, knowing turns into practices, practices become habits, and habits become a part of how we live our lives as worshipers. We become more attuned to God throughout the day. We spend time with him, both in our devotional life and in the mundane moments that make up living. We sing, pray, listen, be still. We "rejoice always, pray continually, give thanks in all circumstances" (1 Thessalonians 5:16-18). We become obedient, humble, faithful. We learn to live a life shaped by his law, remain in his love, and seek his face. We express our love through acts of kindness, both large and small. We learn in greater and greater ways to clothe the naked, feed the hungry, serve the poor, work for the oppressed, do justice, and love mercy, knowing that all these actions and attitudes toward others are also actions and attitudes toward God. In what we do—the work we accomplish and the things we create—we learn to give the glory not to ourselves but to God. We learn to feel God smiling on us as we create, labor, and produce for his glory.

We become a hallelujah, an unceasing outpouring of worship, every day of the week.

WORSHIP PRACTICE

Breath prayer is a spiritual practice in which a short phrase, often a portion of a Bible verse, is repeated in an effort to focus attention back to God. Breath prayer can be employed in two ways: in a repeated fashion during specific times of prayer or internally throughout the day.[4]

As your suggested practice, prayerfully pick a phrase that's meaningful to you. I like to use a portion of the Lord's Prayer: "Thy kingdom come, thy will be done." Say the prayer in your head, and as you do so, attach it to the physical act of breathing. Inhale during the first part of the prayer, and exhale during the second part. Much of what we do as humans is related to muscle memory (from brushing our teeth to driving a car to playing the piano), and the more you attach the prayer to your breathing, the more natural it will become. As you say it over and over throughout the circumstances of your day, it will help you be aware of God's presence with you.

Ten

IMAGINATION AND THE WORSHIPER

> For in him all things were created: things in heaven
> and on earth, visible and invisible, whether thrones
> or powers or rulers or authorities; all things have
> been created through him and for him. He is before
> all things, and in him all things hold together.
>
> **COLOSSIANS 1:16-17**

IF YOU HAVE LITTLE CHILDREN, you probably understand, in deeply mystical and profound ways, this simple word: LEGOs.

My wife and I have four children, and these little plastic baubles have been a part of our home for over twenty years. Our kids have spent countless hours on the living room floor rummaging through the family LEGO bucket, looking for that perfect piece to complete a pirate ship or a submachine gun. Cars, dinosaurs, spaceships, castles, even entire cities have emerged from this bucket. I can still hear the familiar trinkety sound of plastic stirred by little hands. It's the sound of imagination.

This play doesn't come without a cost. I've stepped on LEGOs with bare feet more times than I can count. There was a time when LEGO pieces were strewn all over the house, camouflaged under furniture, imbedded in the shag carpet, floating in people's salads. We still hear the occasional tell-tale *ka-zing!* when we run the vacuum cleaner.

There is something spiritually formative and healthy in such creative activity. When busy hands snap pieces together with increasing complexity, it's a little like God building the universe, from electrons to atoms to molecules and finally to stars and galaxies. LEGOs allow us to express the *imago Dei*, to reenact the first chapter of Genesis in some small way. We imagine. We create. We sit back. And we declare that it is good.

I believe that a well-formed imagination is a necessary aspect of living as a Christ-follower. Indeed, Jesus said some radical, counterintuitive things that could be understood only if one had a good imagination. The kingdom of God is like a pearl of great price. Faith is like a mustard seed. The bread is my body, and the wine is my blood. Robert Webber points out, "At least one-third of the Bible is poetry," and we may indeed need to foster the hearts of poets to understand the heart of God.[1] To reclaim the fullness of worship in our sanctuaries—and in our souls—we need to rekindle our God-given imaginations.

JUST MY IMAGINATION

Have you ever considered the idea that Jesus has an infinite imagination? Because he does. He might have limited himself in some ways through the confines of his incarnation, but the Bible clearly implies that he saw the world differently than did any other person who ever lived. He spoke like a poet, unraveling the mysteries of the kingdom in metaphorical and often provocative prose. He saw the tax collector and the prostitute and befriended them, and he saw a motley group of fishermen and made them his disciples. His introduction to the Sermon on the Mount is filled with an invitation to imagine a world where the poor and the meek and the mourning were actually blessed (Matthew 5:1-10).

And finally, we know that all things were created through the person of Jesus (John 1:1-3; 1 Corinthians 8:6; Colossians 1:15-17). Think about that for a moment: in the nothingness of the beginning of time, the creative muse of the triune Godhead flowed through the pre-incarnate person of Jesus. *All* things have their being through him—the monarch butterfly, the double helix DNA, the Milky Way galaxy, the blue whale, the aurora borealis, the lilies in the field, the children who came to him. Such was the supernatural and infinite imagination of the Son that everything that was created was created through him.

Imagination is defined as "the faculty of imagining, or of forming mental images or concepts of what is not actually present to the senses," or "the ability to face and resolve difficulties; resourcefulness."[2] We all know what imagination is, and we all have one, but have you ever thought about your imagination in spiritual terms? Have you ever wondered how your imagination relates to your soul? Have you ever wondered why you even have an imagination?

Our imaginations are one very important aspect of what it is to be made in the image of God. Now, our imaginations aren't as vast as God's. Our mortal inventions might appear less profound— Velcro, Fruit Roll-ups, the West Coast offense, accordions, tube socks. Nevertheless, we do have an amazing capacity to imagine and conceptualize and dream, which is a very special and important gift from God.

There are at least two reasons why God gave us imaginations. First, human imagination is necessary for us to accomplish the purposes that God intended for us: to fill and subdue the earth (Genesis 1:26-30). In order to fulfill this cultural mandate, it is necessary to have the ability to imagine and create. Without imagination, there would be no farms and crops, no roads and cities, no systems of government and languages for communication. There would be no civilizations, no institutions, no inventions, no art. Humans would not have survived in the wilderness had it not been for our imaginations. Second, I think God gave us imaginations because he wanted us to have fun, or as the Westminster Catechism states so eloquently, "to glorify God, and to enjoy him forever." For it is only through the intellectual imagination that we are able to know and experience a God who is infinite and eternal.

Charles Sherlock contends that the ancient apologists and theologians had a good understanding of Hellenistic philosophy and believed that knowing God was primarily through the intellect. However, "they saw rational knowing as contemplative and imaginative, a reflective journey in truth." He goes on to say that "the word 'imagination,' a Latinism, reflects this intellectual, yet non-rationalistic, understanding."[3] So imagination was considered an intrinsic part of the intellect, a necessary attribute of knowing an unfathomable God.

Now let me share a few caveats. I am not saying that God is imaginary, and I'm certainly not saying that we should imagine things that aren't true. What I am saying is that our ability to imagine and conceptualize is a necessary part of being able to more fully know the one true God. We can understand him and experience him more fully because our imaginations allow us to do so—in our worship, in our prayers, in our thoughts about him, and in our experiences of him.

Let me give you some examples. Have you ever looked up at the stars on a cloudless night and tried to imagine how big our God is? Have you ever sat on a beach and watched the crashing waves and imagined how powerful God is? Have you ever been in a worship experience and pictured God's grace raining down on you or God's arms enveloping you? Have you ever sat in a forest or a garden and marveled at the intricate beauty of God's creation? Have you ever read or listened to a Bible story and imagined being there within the story—with David against Goliath or Moses crossing the Red Sea? These are examples of how our imaginations help us engage in worship.

And we are also able to *glorify* God through the acts and arts and objects of our imaginations. If you've ever written a song to God, painted a painting to glorify God, taught a children's Bible lesson, designed or built a church building, or done anything inventive or creative for the sake of the kingdom, you've used your imagination to glorify God. Certainly the efforts of our creative imaginations have done much to further the kingdom and to help us connect with God.

SACRAMENTAL ACTIONS

Sacraments are rites or actions of the Christian faith regarded as "an outward sign of an inward grace."[4] Sacraments are identified and practiced differently by various Christian faith traditions.

They typically include baptism and Communion but can extend to matrimony, ordination, anointing, and confession. Some faith traditions consider sacraments to be largely symbolic, while others believe that God manifests himself in special ways through the sacraments. Regardless of tradition or denomination, Christians generally understand that the sacraments—particularly baptism and the Lord's Supper—are holy acts with implications for worship.

In a larger sense, however, any public act in which we encounter the very real presence of Christ can be considered *sacramental*—that is, related to the sacred. In our worship services this can include the lighting of candles, the laying on of hands, foot washing, anointing with oil, and the use of sacramental objects such as Advent wreaths or crosses. Sacramental actions are metaphorical by nature; they symbolize some aspect of the Christian metanarrative. They help us tell God's story through imaginative means. Common physical objects and acts can become vessels of transcendence and holiness. Thus sacramental actions are incarnational in that they are material representations of the spiritual reality.

There is poetry in the act of Communion, as we reenact the profound mystery of Jesus with ordinary table items and encounter the real presence of Jesus. In the shadow of the Passover meal, we eat the bread, we drink the cup, and we proclaim the Lord's death until he comes (1 Corinthians 11:26). There is nuanced symbolism in the waters of baptism, as we are first buried in the waters and then reincarnated out of the waters into new life in Christ. We are washed of our sin in the water; we were born first in water and "born again" in the Spirit. There is visual symbolism in the candle lighting of a Christmas Eve service, as we are reminded that the light of the world is born and that we are to carry that light into the world (John 8:12; Matthew 5:14-16). Even the crosses that hang in our sanctuaries can have deeper meanings when re-visioned through the imagination. In these and in many other sacramental actions and artistic expressions we find the language of imaginative worship.

I truly believe that a sacramental worldview—seeing the entire world as a sacred creation loved by God—is a necessary aspect of fostering the soul of the worshiper. Our imaginations can help attune us to the divine voice. And this should make sense, for what we see is not all there is. There is so much more going on than in what our eyes perceive. Andrew Greeley described the "sacramental" imagination as the ability "to imagine God as present in the world and the world as revelatory instead of bleak."[5] The true reality that Jesus invites us to recognize is the invisible, supernatural world that is all around us. God has placed his kingdom right in front of our eyes, and the glory of God is bursting all around us. We can see it if we only squint hard enough.

Some of us, especially those who are more in the evangelical streams, have lost this sense of imagination in our services. We've all seen instances when worship has devolved into singing and the sermon has devolved into studying. But there is much more that we can do to involve our imaginations in worship. We can tell more stories, use more metaphorical language, incorporate more symbols and imagery, embrace sacramental actions, sing more songs with poetic lyrics, contemplate and visualize and imagine. We can give ourselves permission to worship with our imaginations. We can move beyond mere propositional worship and into a fuller kingdom-oriented worship.

Recently, my church invited one of the spiritual directors in our congregation to lead us during worship in a visualization prayer exercise. After some musical worship, she invited everyone to sit quietly and place a picture of themselves as a child in their mind. Perhaps it was a baby photo or a childhood memory. As we held that image in our minds, she invited us to imagine what God thought of that child. What were God's hopes for that young person? What were his feelings? How much did God love that child? In the contemplative silence of that moment, I believe the Spirit of God reminded us that we are all his children, beloved and deeply embraced in his arms.

IMAGINATION AND FAITH

Now let me take this one step further. I contend that imagination is a necessary component of faith. For "faith is the assurance of things hoped for, the conviction of things not seen" (Hebrews 11:1 NASB), and the first step of faith is by definition a step into the unseen, the unknown.

Noah needed to exercise his imagination in order to build his great boat. Abraham and Sarah needed to exercise their imaginations when God told them they would be parents of a vast family. Nehemiah needed to exercise his imagination in order to rebuild the walls of Jerusalem. The apostle John needed no small exercise in imagination when he was moved to write the book of Revelation. Acts of faith, both great and small, often require some aspect of imagination, some act of thinking beyond what we can simply see with our eyes.

Have you ever been in a situation where God called you to do something that you thought was crazy, or at least a little weird? Have you ever had a build-an-ark moment? Has God ever given you a vision for a ministry, or for a career, or for a church? Or maybe something more personal, like a vision for your future, or your marriage, or your children, or a single moment in time? In such instances we must "live by faith, not by sight" (2 Corinthians 5:7). Indeed, life is full of opportunities for us to exercise our faith, and in kind, our imaginations. If faith really is the substance of things unseen, then this must be true.

There's an interesting passage in the Gospels where Jesus interacts with some children. Jesus not only attracted masses of people, but he attracted the youngsters as well. Among all his important preaching and healing, some of the people began to bring their children forward, asking to receive a blessing from Jesus. But the disciples felt that Jesus was too important, too busy to have these kids getting in the way. They began to shoo them off.

But Jesus stopped them. And looking down at the boys and girls, the little ones, Jesus said something quite remarkable and countercultural and completely fundamental to the idea of faith. Jesus said, "Let the little children come to me, and do not hinder them, for the kingdom of heaven belongs to such as these" (Matthew 19:14). This is the same kingdom of heaven that Jesus referred to in the Beatitudes when he said, "Blessed are the poor in spirit, for theirs is the kingdom of heaven" (Matthew 5:3). What I believe he was saying was that a person's faith must be pure and certain and trusting, like that of a child. Not to be childish (for that is a fool's faith), but to be childlike (which is to have a confident and secure trust). You reach your hand out to the hand of a child, and the child will implicitly know that you will safely walk them across the street.

Perhaps this is one of the reasons why Jesus encouraged us to have the faith of a child. It is easy for children to believe that sponges can talk, superheroes can fly, Tin Men can have hearts, and the safest place to be is on their parent's lap. They have the natural ability to suspend their cynicisms, their false paradigms, and their small realities and exercise their God-given imaginations, exercise their faith. Imagination helps us to see that there is much more than meets the eye. It can help us see that anything is possible in a world where God is in control. It allows us to engage more deeply in the story of God and our place in it. It allows us to dream big dreams. And it is a necessary component of childlike faith.

When my children were very little, it was common for them to dream about cartoon characters. They were always excited to share their dreams with me, dreams where real people and things interacted naturally with cartoons, like a scene from *Mary Poppins*. But as they grew older, they lost the ability to dream about their cartoon friends. They lost the ability to imagine, even in their dreams. Perhaps we must push back against the folly of our advanced age and strive to recapture our imaginations—in our lives, in our faith, in our worship.

WORSHIP PRACTICE

As we close this chapter, I'd like to invite you into an exercise of imagination in worship. For some this may appear odd or even uncomfortable. But really, this is no different from reading a story.

First, assume a relaxed posture, both physically and mentally. Second, ask God to meet you and inspire you in the words of this story (based on Matthew 14:22-33). Third, read the following passage slowly and deliberately, like sipping a cup of hot tea. Or have someone read it for you and just close your eyes. Finally, give yourself permission to simply *imagine*.

You're weary and worn from an extremely long day of ministry. It was an emotional day, filled with amazing events that you will talk about for the rest of your life. But for now, all your body wants is a little rest. The sun is already setting on the Sea of Galilee as you and several tired men launch out on your boat. Soon the sun sets, and you are left in the darkened haze somewhere miles from the Capernaum shore. Suddenly, a strong wind begins to blow your little boat. The buffeting continues, first slowly and then violently. As you are tossed by the increasing waves and pounded by the wind, one of the men yells, "Grab an oar! Make for the shore!" You grab an oar and begin pulling at it frantically. You and the others strain against the water, paddling into the blackness. You fight against the roughened sea for what seems to be hours. And then, without warning, an apparition appears above the waters.

"It is a ghost!" one cries out. Deprived of sleep and weary from your rowing, you are gripped by a sudden terror. It is a

deep and conscious fear that slips inside your bones like a cold shiver. In the distance you see the figure of a man, cloaked in the darkness and treading the surging waves.

"Do not fear," comes a voice from the mysterious figure. "It is I." Fearful, frazzled, exhausted, you immediately recognize it to be your teacher, your friend. It is Jesus the Nazarene. Your fear turns to dumbfounded awe.

This is incredible. Beyond reason. Beyond rationale. Beyond the very physical laws of nature. But there he is. Jesus appears on the waters to his disciples. Simon, sitting next to you, is the first to speak. Simon, the bold and often impulsive one, challenges the voice. "If it is really you, then tell me to come to you on the water." And Jesus' simple response is "Come."

You want to grab Simon and keep him from jumping out of the boat, but you are too dumbfounded to act on your thoughts. With equal parts caution and recklessness, Simon steps out of the boat and carefully places his foot on the ebbing surface of the deep expanse. He tests it, and finds it solid and secure under his sandal. Emboldened now, he stands beside the boat, his feet firm on the foamy sea, his eyes firmly on Jesus. And then, to the amazement of the other disciples, he walks—one step at a time—upon the waters.

Now, you know Simon. You know he's just a simple man, maybe a little impulsive, but he's a good guy, sincere and passionate. So you realize that he probably doesn't fully comprehend the incomprehensibility of that moment. He is simply doing the impossible—walking on water. But he can only take this suspension of disbelief so far. With the wind in his face and the waves lapping at his feet, he begins to lose heart. He begins to sink into the dark water.

And that is when Jesus grabs him. That is when Jesus saves him.

You realize only now in this moment how tightly you are holding on to the edge of the boat. You breathe a sigh of relief as you watch Simon and Jesus slowly make their way back through the wind-swept waves and into your fragile wooden vessel. And suddenly, immediately, as quick as the wave of a hand, the wind dies down to a whisper.

Silence. You no longer hear the waves slapping the boat, the wind wailing against your ears. You no longer feel the mist against your face or the fear grip your soul. You now hear only the beating of your heart and the silence of the moment.

There is only one thing to do now. You bow your head. And you worship your friend, this man from Nazareth, whose name is Jesus.

Eleven

COMPASSION AND JUSTICE

> He has told you, O man, what is good;
> And what does the LORD require of you
> But to do justice, to love kindness,
> And to walk humbly with your God?
>
> MICAH 6:8 NASB

IT WAS A TYPICAL SACRAMENTO FALL MORNING—one of those days when a cold, white fog hangs in the air like a wet blanket. I had been on full-time staff as the worship pastor at my church for about a year. I was young, well-intentioned, naive, and busy doing something I'm sure I thought was important at the time. That's when he walked in.

He was about six foot two. Tall, thin, wearing dirty, baggy clothes, bundled in a stained denim jacket and carrying an army duffle bag—the young man had scraggly hair and a tired, broken-down look on his face. He looked like a transient. A "bum." As he strode through the main office door, I subconsciously put myself on the defensive. *Who is this guy? Why is he here? What are his intentions?*

Despite my suspicions, he greeted me politely and asked if the church had an extra Bible he could have. As I watched him fumble for words, I noticed something in his eyes. A tiredness. A sadness. A searching. So we started to talk.

He told me he was living behind one of the grocery stores in town, eating the stale doughnuts that the bakery tossed out. He didn't have a place to go, and he had no one to go with. We talked briefly, and I gave him a Bible. And then, for reasons I didn't understand, I felt the urge to do something more. Before I knew what I was doing, I took out a pen and scrawled my home phone number on the back of a business card. I handed it to him and told him to call if he needed help.

As he left, I said two prayers: first, a prayer for his protection and safety, and second, a selfish prayer that I will never forget. *Please God, don't let him call me. You have no idea how busy I am right now.*

Since that time, I've learned never to pray prayers like that.

That evening, I received a phone call from the man, wondering whether I could offer him a place to stay. As I drove over to the grocery store to get him, I thought, *What are you getting yourself into? This guy could stab you, rob you, throw you in the river, steal your stuff, hurt your kids.* But there was something about this that I could not ignore. Somehow I felt that God was in it. This was something God wanted me to do. So I picked him up and brought him into my house to meet my wife and my children, to sit at my table and eat my food, to sleep under my roof.

I'll always be thankful that I have a wife who trusts me in these things, because I know she was as unsure as I was as to how this was going to pan out. But she and I fed him, allowed him to take a long, hot bath, gave him a place to sleep, and washed his clothes. That night, we listened to his story, helped him through his tears, prayed with him. And sometime that night, this transient became a person to me.

John (not his real name) was a professional boxer at the back end of his career. At one time he had been a ranked WBA fighter, but time had started to catch up with him. He was the son of devoted Seventy-day Adventists, and his father had been a sparring partner for George Foreman. John had gotten caught up in a web of relationships with people who were heavily into drugs, and he had a bad marriage and three children. Through all the incredibly bad luck he was having and the incredibly bad life decisions he was making, he decided to head out onto the streets. He had ended up at our church by chance. He simply wasn't paying attention to where he was walking.

Looking back now, I don't know what God's plan was, but I know he was up to something. I felt that God was tugging at John hard, tugging at him to make major changes in his life. But what I didn't see was how God was changing me, changing my perspective, forcing me to see people the way he sees people—with kindness, goodness, mercy, and love.

After a week or so of giving John rides, buying him some clothes and boots, and just trying to be his friend, he ended up calling his parents and reestablishing his relationship with them. He started making better decisions—socially, vocationally, spiritually. We even visited his extended family and hometown church, and our children played with his children at his parents' home. You see, somewhere in all of this, John had become a friend.

The irony in this story doesn't escape me. At the time, I was doing so much for the kingdom of God that I didn't see the kingdom right in front of me. I was so busy trying to do God's work, I hadn't taken the time to see the world through God's eyes. Ultimately it was an issue of honest worship. How could I presume to lead people to worship a God of grace and compassion if I didn't allow his grace and compassion to flow through me? If I was to worship God with all that I am, shouldn't my heart be aligned to his?

God placed a man in my life, and he gave me an opportunity to be used in a small way. God wanted me to invite this stranger beyond my comfort zones—into my home, into my life. And in the God-ordained intersection of our two stories, neither his life nor mine would ever be the same.

LIVING IT OUT

Jesus, in accordance with Scripture, linked worship with compassion and justice when he taught that the great commandment— "Love the Lord your God with all your heart and with all your soul and with all your mind"—was related to the Golden Rule: "Love your neighbor as yourself" (Matthew 22:36-40). In other words, our love for God should extend to the people God loves. God's people are intended to be a practical expression of God's love in the way they love each other and the world. Clearly a life of worship—loving God with our whole self—is a life concerned with the needs and struggles of our neighbor.

But reality is often different. We are mortal beings after all. We can earnestly and wholeheartedly sing God's praises on Sunday morning and then swear at the traffic on the way home from church. We can post Scripture passages on Facebook along with insensitive religious rants. We can sing, "Bless the Lord, O my soul," but not take the time to reorient our lives to bless the poor, the needy, the broken. But Jesus warned us that such actions have consequences.

> When the Son of Man comes in his glory, and all the angels with him, he will sit on his glorious throne. All the nations will be gathered before him, and he will separate the people one from another as a shepherd separates the sheep from the goats. He will put the sheep on his right and the goats on his left.
>
> Then the King will say to those on his right, "Come, you who are blessed by my Father; take your inheritance, the kingdom prepared for you since the creation of the world. For I was hungry and you gave me something to eat, I was thirsty and you gave me something to drink, I was a stranger and you invited me in, I needed clothes and you clothed me, I was sick and you looked after me, I was in prison and you came to visit me." . . .
>
> The King will reply, "Truly I tell you, whatever you did for one of the least of these brothers and sisters of mine, you did for me." (Matthew 25:31-36, 40)

These are strong words. Worship requires a heart that is aligned with God's heart. Worship that isn't concerned for the least of these—worship that doesn't advocate for justice, love, and peace—is rejected by God as self-focused, even false. The great commandment is always linked with the Golden Rule because God's kingdom and his story is at its essence a story of justice and redemption. For "anyone who loves God must also love their brother and sister" (1 John 4:21).

The trend to create missions ministries and committees as a separate arm of the church has had unintended consequences. In our Western paradigms, worship and mission seem quite separate. But obviously Jesus did not see it this way. When Jesus coupled the great commandment with the Golden Rule, he recognized that how we treat God and how we treat others come from the same place: our souls. Our actions emanate from who we are. Once again, it is an issue of honest worship. As disciples of Jesus whose lives are continually being transformed, all our relationships should naturally be affected. Immersed in the truth and reality of God's redemptive story, we become active participants in redemption, not only for ourselves but also for others. In other words, a worshiping life is fueled by grace, demonstrates compassion, and works for justice. If we're pursuing the depths of God, we must also pursue our neighbors. For if we have the heart of God, we hear their cries.

These days the word *justice* is both fashionable and misunderstood. It has been appropriated by a number of different social and political agendas, so there's some baggage associated with it. But it's a good word, a biblical word, so perhaps a definition is in order. Justice can be defined as a use of power in accordance with the nature of God. In other words, justice is power used to bring love, goodness, and redemption to those with less power, rather than harm, abuse, and neglect.

We all have power at some level. We have the power to criticize or compliment, the power to enact or neglect, the power to be generous or miserly. We can sow justice through the things we buy, through the politics we support, through the charities we contribute to, through the ministries we serve in, and especially through the way we treat people—friends and strangers, rich and poor, adults and children, people halfway around the world and the people who live in our own home.

Jesus, the most powerful human who ever walked this planet, is our model for justice. We can see this in how he treated those with little power—the poor, the meek, the disenfranchised, the foreigner. We are to love the world as he loved the world and gave himself for us.

JUSTICE IN THE CHURCH

In *The Dangerous Act of Worship*, Mark Labberton writes,

> The stark track record of the contemporary American church, however, seems to be that the plight of the poor and suffering have only a tertiary connection at best with our pursuit of worship. It is meant to have a primary place, as it does in the heart of God. . . . The perception that issues of worship and issues of justice are separate or sequential or easily distinguishable shows the inadequacy of our theology, both of worship and of justice.[1]

I've found this to be often true. In many churches, worship is an "in here" thing, and feeding and clothing the poor is an "out there" thing. But the two are more entwined than we know. Indeed, as worshipers we must diligently push back against the idea that these are dichotomous actions, for Jesus implied that the heart that loves God and the heart that loves others must be one and the same. Consider the words of Isaiah:

> When you come to appear before me [says the Lord],
> who has asked this of you,

this trampling of my courts?
Stop bringing meaningless offerings!
Your incense is detestable to me.
New Moons, Sabbaths and convocations—
I cannot bear your worthless assemblies.
Your New Moon feasts and your appointed festivals
I hate with all my being.
They have become a burden to me;
I am weary of bearing them.
When you spread out your hands in prayer,
I hide my eyes from you;
even when you offer many prayers,
I am not listening.

Your hands are full of blood!

Wash and make yourselves clean.
Take your evil deeds out of my sight;
stop doing wrong.
Learn to do right; seek justice.
Defend the oppressed.
Take up the cause of the fatherless;
plead the case of the widow. (Isaiah 1:12-17)

The meaning is plain and gravely consequential. God rejects worship from hearts that don't seek righteousness or show compassion. Such worship is meaningless and detestable, worthless assemblies that God can't bear. For "righteousness and justice are the foundation of your throne; love and faithfulness go before you" (Psalm 89:14). We worship before a throne built on righteousness and justice. I agree with Labberton—with fear and trembling—when he describes worship as a "dangerous act." For we are in danger of offering a holy and almighty God detestable worship.

But now consider the positive side of this passage. Imagine worship that is practiced by souls that care for the poor, engage in actions of compassion, give generously to agencies and charities that care for the disenfranchised and needy, serve in foster homes and food banks and prison ministries, and pray, "Thy kingdom come, thy will be done." Imagine soul worship by those who do right and seek justice, defend the oppressed and care for the fatherless and widow. Imagine worship that comes from hearts that are aligned to God's heart—worship that is honest and true. Truly this is worship that pleases our Lord.

The first-century church was a powerful thing. It was an alternative community, a place where slaves and masters, men and women, Greeks and Jews interacted radically in loving community to one another and out to others—the strangers, the widows, and the orphans. Their loving actions for one another and for the world were a testimony to the redemptive power of Jesus. "And the Lord added to their number daily" (Acts 2:47).[2] This is the type of worship that truly changed the world. When we speak of Jesus but we don't treat others with compassion and justice, our gospel rings hollow to the world. But when we do live out our love and devotion to Jesus with compassion and justice, we become instruments of shalom.[3]

My home church is in an affluent area in Northern California. That said, there are people in my congregation who have experienced Majority World poverty, people who have been released from prison, people who are in twelve-step programs, people who are widows and orphans, people who have been affected by the sex-trafficking trade, people who subsist on food stamps, people who have experienced homelessness, and people who came from oppressed family environments. So actions of justice and compassion aren't just "out there" things. And they are more than "in here" as well. When we worship, we worship *with* the least of these. For the least of these is also a very valued and loved part of the bride of Christ.

Our worship, both personal and corporate, must align with God's heart for compassion and justice. Once again, it's a question of integrity. To worship is also to do justice, to love kindness, and to walk humbly with God (Micah 6:8).

MORE TO THE STORY

Time passed, and the increasing pace of life made John a distant memory—until I received a newspaper clipping in the mail from an anonymous sender. It was an article about a tall, thin, light heavyweight boxer who was out on a morning jog. According to the story, the man saw smoke pouring out of a neighborhood house, so he ran to the burning building, knocked in a window, and saved the family inside. It was my friend John. The man God had brought into our lives many years before. The man who had been very far away from God. But by God's good grace, he had come back home.

Now, I've never saved anyone from a burning building, but I think about the fact that John might not have been there to save those people if I hadn't been there for him. I'm no hero like John. But I'm very grateful that God tugged on me that day, stirring my heart to align with his. I'm grateful God decided to share his un-conditional love with John through me and through my family. And I'm grateful God transformed my heart in some small way through John.

I'd like to think that's what happens when you and I begin to have the soul of a worshiper.

WORSHIP PRACTICE

Lectio divina is a spiritual practice of reading a passage of Scripture slowly and deliberately, not for the sake of studying the passage but for allowing the passage to speak into you. To practice lectio divina, first put yourself in a quiet and attentive posture, allowing the Spirit to speak to you. Put yourself in a posture of surrender to the truth of God. Slowly read Matthew 25:31-40, one sentence at a time, pausing between sentences. When you're finished, ponder the meanings for a moment. Then read it again. And read it again. What words stand out to you? What might be God's invitation to you? Over the course of your reading, see if you're being prompted by the Spirit to think of a person, situation, ministry, or action. What is God speaking to you in this passage?

Twelve

THE DEEP END OF THE POOL

Now it was a river that I could not cross, because
the water had risen and was deep enough to
swim in—a river that no one could cross. He
asked me, "Son of man, do you see this?"

EZEKIEL 47:5-6

I HAVE A FEAR OF WATER. It's not that I don't know how to swim; it's that I have an irrational fear, a mild form of aquaphobia. I think it stems from my mom, who wanted to make sure we didn't venture too close to the swimming pool when we were little. She planted the fear of water into us so deeply, my three brothers and I all have this same phobia. And I still feel the irrational fear when I'm in a pool and I can feel myself drifting into the deep end. My pulse quickens, my breaths shorten, my hands tremble, my peripheral vision closes in to a tunnel of fear.

When I was in college, I went camping with some friends, and we came across a large stream that pooled into a swimming hole, complete with a small waterfall that served as a makeshift high dive. It was picturesque. But there was no way I was going to jump into the pool with everyone else. As an excuse, I told a few people I'd rather explore downstream.

As I hiked by that fast-moving stream, I stepped on some wet moss on the rocks. Suddenly I slid on a large granite slab that dumped me squarely into the river. The biting cold water startled me, and immediately my body went into full panic. I began flailing, trying to get my bearings, but I was sucking in water involuntarily. Everything started closing in on me, and then my consciousness went into slow motion, as my young life flashed before my eyes, like a dream sequence in a bad movie.

In the midst of all the tossing and turning, bubbles and gurgling and flashbacks, I heard shouting, far off in the distance. Someone was calling my name, and yes, I could hear a little reverb. "Manuel! Manuel!" the voice cried out. "Stand up!"

I stopped flailing long enough to realize I was in three feet of water. As I stood to my feet, dripping and embarrassed, I saw all my friends looking down at me from the bank like I was a crazy person. Which I am. Maybe we all are.

WATER FROM THE TEMPLE

Ezekiel 47, the final oracle of the prophet, describes the river that flows from the temple. In this last dramatic vision, Ezekiel pictures the glory of the Lord fully inhabiting a restored temple, a restored Jerusalem, and a restored people. This vision includes a river that springs from the temple and gushes all the way to the Dead Sea. So while most of the book has a foreboding, somber tone, it's ultimately a book about hope. In a way, it's laid out like an epic movie, filled with heartache and trials, but ultimately ending in triumph. God's triumph.

In the vision, Ezekiel is accompanied by a heavenly guide (perhaps an angel) who wishes to reveal the future Jerusalem and the future temple to him. He's like a tour guide, and I can picture him excited to show what God will do. "Look over here," I can hear him say. "See the new temple. Isn't this amazing? Isn't this just the way of our God?" I can picture the guide taking Ezekiel from the inner court gate facing east to the sacred rooms in the north to the outer court and all four corners, then back to the temple. And all the while, he's motioning to Ezekiel as if to say, "Behold! Behold the glory of the Lord!"

And then Ezekiel sees it.

Inexplicably, water is flowing freely from under the threshold of the temple. The guide leads him out, following the water, which flows east. As if to impress Ezekiel with the size, he takes measurements as they go. At a thousand cubits, which is over a quarter of a mile, the water is ankle deep. At two thousand cubits, it's knee-deep. At three thousand cubits, it's up to the waist. At four thousand cubits—which is now over a mile from the temple—the water is so deep, he can no longer ford it. It's too deep and too fast to cross. The stream that started as a trickle ends as a swollen river.

And that's not all. The stream begins to fill and refresh the Dead Sea. Saltwater becomes fresh. Fish teem wherever the water fills it. Fruit trees blossom on the banks. There are so many fish and other life in the sea that fishermen wouldn't even have to put out into the water. They'd be able to cast their nets right from the banks. It's like the ending scene in *The Lion King*, where the ecosystem is restored to God's original intention. It's an Eden again. What a glorious vision!

We take it for granted that water runs out showerheads and fills swimming pools. We turn the faucet on, and water automatically comes. We sit down at a restaurant, and the server places a glass of water in front of us. It's easy to take water for granted. But water meant something very different in the time and place of the biblical writers. Water was life. Water meant that you could grow food, you could drink, you could fish, you could cook, you could survive. In that arid part of the world, water was life. So water meant flourishing, thriving, prospering.

For Ezekiel, water meant even more. He was prophesying during a terrible time in the history of the Jewish people. Both Jerusalem and the temple had been devastated. The Israelites were scattered, living in foreign lands or in poverty in their own ruined land. The structures of their civilization, including the royal line, were gone. And then he saw this new vision—a vision of the glory of the Lord entering the temple and reestablishing his will and kingdom. A miraculous river flowed from the altar, flowing and rising, widening and deepening, refreshing the land even to the point of reviving the Dead Sea. It's also significant that it flowed from the temple, the place of sacrifice, a sacramental spot on which God and his people made amends.

What does the water represent here in Ezekiel 47? Commentaries differ. Some say that it signifies the gospel of Christ. Some imply it represents the gifts and power of the Holy Spirit. And more generally, the water represents God's kingdom blessing on the land. Some state that it's literal: an actual river will erupt from the temple, finding its way all the way to the Dead Sea. There are disagreements about how literally or figuratively the water should be interpreted, but I don't think these different interpretations contradict one another in the big picture. It's obvious that Ezekiel is referring to the redemptive action of God for the land and more importantly for his people.

SUNDAY BONNETS OR CRASH HELMETS

Prophecy often works on more than one level. Of course, it applied to the nation Israel and served as a promise to God's people for his future rescue and blessing. Think about the nation Israel, downtrodden and oppressed, and the promise of a river that flows from the temple threshold and revives even the Dead Sea. Whether literal or symbolic, it speaks to a reconciled and rejuvenated future. It speaks of hope. It speaks of God's future reign and sovereignty. But it also works for us today, in the here and now.

We gather on a Sunday morning, in our sanctuaries, among our fellow congregants, and it's a good thing. There's a comfortableness on a Sunday morning, a sense of peace in the midst of an unnerving, confusing world. You sit in your normal spot, among people you know and surroundings that are familiar and comforting. And that's a good thing, experiencing the peace of community in God's presence and with God's people. But comfort sometimes lends itself to casualness. And casualness can sometimes lead to laxity and indifference.

This should not be so. For in its essence worship is an extraordinary, astounding, mind-boggling act. In worship the God of creation, the God of almighty power and might, the God who spins the atoms and sustains the universe by his active will, is *actually* here. And if he really is here, in his manifest presence, why aren't we all on our faces, trembling in holy fear, hands raised and heads bowed, slain where we stand?

Annie Dillard said it better:

> On the whole, I do not find Christians, outside of the catacombs, sufficiently sensible of conditions. Does anyone have the foggiest idea what sort of power we so blithely invoke? Or, as I suspect, does no one believe a word of it? The churches are children playing on the floor with their chemistry sets, mixing up a batch of TNT to kill a Sunday morning. It is madness to wear ladies' straw hats and velvet hats to church; we should all be wearing crash helmets. Ushers should issue life preservers and signal flares; they should lash us to our pews.[1]

When we gather on Sunday morning, we're ushered into the presence and power of God. And we have a choice. We can go the first thousand cubits and wade into worship up to our ankles. Or we can choose to go another thousand cubits and experience worship up to our knees. Or we can take those extra steps to where we're experiencing worship up to our waists. Or we can go the full mile in our worship experience, traveling the entire four thousand cubits into the scary, untamed water, the torrent too deep and too fast to cross.

When we show up late to church, when we give an obligatory sleepy nod to worship, when we float halfheartedly in and out from our seats in a spiritual yawning, we reveal what we truly believe about God. It's like we're sitting in the kiddy pool, content to splash in six inches of water.

One of the aspects of falling on your face in worship is that you're struck by a holy, reverent fear. Our shock and awe justified. Our God is fearsome and mighty, the One who makes the mountains tremble, the seas roar, the galaxies spiral, and every atom in the universe spin. Truly there is something going on in our sanctuaries and worship spaces that is supernatural, mysterious, unfathomable. When we gather to worship, we come face to face with the eternal, manifest presence of the great I Am. God beckons us into the deep waters, into the fast-moving currents of his holiness. The thought of it should make our pulses quicken, our breaths shorten, our hands shake, our peripheral vision close in to a tunnel of holy fear and reverence.

So we stand by the banks of the river, the rushing stream swirling in currents mysterious and unfathomable. Above the tumult of the water's roar, the Lord beckons us in his still, small voice.

He walks on these deep waters. And he beckons us to walk with him.

WORSHIP PRACTICE

Do we *really* believe that God is with us as we worship? The next time you're participating in corporate worship, use your imagination to picture God there before you, seated on his throne, active and involved, beckoning you closer in, deeper still. Keep this image of God throughout your worship time, and see if it affects how you interact with God during the worship experience.

BENEDICTION

THROUGHOUT THE WRITING OF THIS BOOK, it was my hope that it might make a difference, not just in the actions of the worshiper but deep in the soul as well. I'm hopeful that we might be able to thirst more powerfully for God and to wade into the deeper waters of worship. I'm hopeful for our churches, our congregations, the people of God. And I'm hopeful that we might be able to reclaim our souls for him.

The book of Numbers has a very hopeful blessing that I would like to leave you with. It's the blessing that Aaron, at Moses' direction, pronounced upon the people of God, and it is often used as a benediction at the end of worship services as a reminder that we take the goodness of God with us. I thought it appropriate that we end the book with these words as my prayer for you as you go forth in worship.

> The LORD bless you and keep you;
> The LORD make His face shine upon you,
> And be gracious to you;
> The LORD lift up His countenance upon you,
> And give you peace. (Numbers 6:24-26 NKJV)

ACKNOWLEDGMENTS

MUCH LIKE THE PARABLE OF THE STONE SOUP, the many principles, concepts, and musings in this book have been blended and stewed from a wide variety of sources, some of which are listed in the endnotes and many more of which came from life experiences and lessons learned long ago. Perhaps the meatiest of the ingredients come from those theologians, philosophers, and apologists who have come before us to set our path. But the seasoning and spice definitely comes from the many people God has placed in my life, those who have influenced me in ways I cannot even begin to comprehend.

I am indebted to those who have reviewed or influenced various iterations of my manuscript: Eric Aiston, Judi Alexander, Teresa Harbert, Kevin Houk, Steve Liberti, Valerie Harrison, Tim and Claire Marker, Dan Maust, Cate Morris, Lorraine Rothenburg, Ted and Ashley Hansen, Dr. W. David O. Taylor, and my patient editor, Cindy Bunch. Your kind reflections and comments have been helpful and life giving.

I also acknowledge the many worship pastors and leaders I've known throughout the years, those quiet heroes who have given their imperfect best to the people of God for his glory. May we all find ourselves together one day before the throne offering the worship of our greatest aspirations.

Acknowledgments

I am extremely grateful to the fellowship of Oak Hills Church in Folsom, California, and particularly my pastors, Kent Carlson and Mike Lueken, the staff and leadership, and especially the many talented and gracious people in our IMPACT worship and arts ministries. Oak Hills has been our worship laboratory for decades, and this book could not have been lived out and written without you all.

Finally, I've heard it said that behind every great man is a woman rolling her eyes. My love and appreciation to my supportive and gracious wife, Debbie, and to our amazing children, Eric, Justin, Rachel, and Paige. I have learned as much about the nature of our Abba God and our relationship with him by being a father and a husband as from any hundred books I've read.

DISCUSSION GUIDE

THESE DISCUSSION QUESTIONS are intended to create dialogue in a small group setting. If you're in a discussion group, I encourage you not to use this forum to be judgmental, argumentative, or comparative, but instead seek to understand, empathize, and foster the heart of a learner. Also, it would be better to choose two or three questions and go deep rather than to discuss all of them in a cursory way. At the end of your time, pray the suggested prayer, either individually or as a group.

CHAPTER 1: HOLY SMOKE

1. Describe the type and style of church service you attend. Is it big or small, modern or traditional, technology-driven or unplugged? What is your involvement in your church?

2. How would you define transcendence? Can you share an instance when you felt a sense of transcendence, either through music and the arts or in some other way?

3. This book describes spectacle and transcendence as two different things. Have you experienced spectacle without transcendence? Have you experienced transcendence without spectacle? How are they related, and how are they different?

4. Are there any "golden calves" in your life, either now or previously? What were those things or people, outside of God, that you revered or even worshiped?

5. Discuss the concept that human beings are made to worship. Do you believe this to be true?

6. In your own words, what is the role of the Holy Spirit as it relates to worship?

7. According to this chapter, the true "product" of church ministry is the hearts of the people, and a "byproduct" is what happens on stage. Do you agree or disagree? Is this congruous with your church experiences?

Suggested prayer. Pray that God would reveal those areas in your worship that are driven more by your agendas than by God's holiness and that Spirit-driven transcendence would be the basis for your worship.

CHAPTER 2: FIRST-PERSON SINGULAR

1. List some examples of cultural narcissism that you have personally experienced or seen around you (advertising, television, social media, etc.).

2. Of the things on your list from the previous question, do you relate to any of them personally? How has cultural narcissism affected you?

3. "Cultural narcissism is in direct conflict with the gospel." What are some practical ways in which you can be more purposeful in resisting the forces of cultural narcissism? What's one practical thing you can do, as a spiritual practice, to push back against our current society?

4. Have you ever found yourself rating the worship during a service? Do you make judgments about the music, performers, sermon, or programs? When is it legitimate and when is it not legitimate to do so?

5. How do you define "good" worship?

6. Do you see ways cultural narcissism has crept into your worship, either in your personal devotions or in your worship services? How?

7. The next time you're worshiping, be aware of your spiritual posture. Do you have a "me" attitude during worship? Are you focused inwardly on your experience of the worship or outwardly to God? Make it your intention to please God through your worship, and not yourself.

Suggested prayer. Ask God to reveal areas in your life where you may be more affected by cultural narcissism than you're aware. It could be in your attitude toward others, your need to judge and evaluate and have your needs met, or your attitude in worship. Make it your prayer to be "one who has clean hands and a pure heart."

CHAPTER 3: FALLING ON MY FACE

The discussion questions in this chapter have been split into two sections: one for everyone, and one specifically for vocational pastors and ministers.

For everyone.

1. "Pride is the universal sin of exalting ourselves and placing our own interests above the interests of others." Are there

areas of your life where pride is an issue? Hint: If the answer is no, you may have an issue with pride. Seriously, pride is seldom obvious but more often subtle and under the surface. Examples can be small yet point to larger issues. Where are areas where you deal with pride?

2. Define humility in your own words. How does that compare with the working definition of humility mentioned in this chapter? How do you think this definition helps us in our quest in worship?

3. Would you describe yourself as having genuine humility? Would your family and close friends? Why or why not? What are the humility barriers in your life?

4. "While our relationship with Jesus is personal, it is not intended to be private." Worship is generally to be experienced in community. How can you make your Sunday worship experience a more community-oriented one?

For pastors, ministers, and church leaders.

1. Chapter three mentions that there are unique pressures and expectations on the pastorate. Do you resonate with any of these issues? If so, how?

2. Do you have people with whom you can be transparent about your struggles, challenges, and humanity? If so, how does that help you? If it doesn't help, why?

3. Would you characterize your personal ministry style as having genuine humility? Would your congregation? Why or why not?

Suggested prayer. Ask God to reveal areas in which you need to grow in humility. As we work through the rest of the book, we'll learn more about how to deal with these issues.

CHAPTER 4: THE NATURE OF IDENTITY

This chapter is a can of worms, and sometimes discussion groups don't have the intimacy and trust required to tackle some of the deeper issues. If you're in a small group, give yourselves permission to discuss this chapter in conceptual terms, not speaking personally unless everyone feels comfortable with that. However, this is a critical chapter, and individual depth and transparency may be necessary to move forward in your spiritual walk.

1. Discuss "Some of the Lies of Pride." Do you resonate with any of the lies? How do you see them in yourself or in others? How can the lies affect our worship? (Note: We will discuss this in greater detail in chapter five.)

2. How do you see yourself? Choose four or five adjectives that you think describe who you are. Write them down, but don't share them. Are there any words on your list that people may be surprised to see if they read them? This is a comparison between the first and second persona: who you think you are versus who you portray yourself to be.

3. How do people see you? Ask a few people you know, or your discussion group, to write down four or five adjectives that they think describe you and then share them with you. Are there words on their lists that surprise you? Are there words that confirm who you think you are? This is a comparison between the first and third persona: who

you think you are versus who people actually see when they experience you.

4. Discuss the fourth persona, who God sees. Who does God believe you to be? Take time to look up the Scripture passages referenced on page 59.

Suggested prayer. Pray that the Holy Spirit would help you be self-discerning and allow you to break through whatever self-deceptions you may have. Pray the fourth persona over yourself, reminding yourself of how God sees you—as his dearly beloved child.

CHAPTER 5: WORSHIP FROM THE TRUE SELF

1. Imagine that, in the thick of an ordinary day, you had a "woman at the well" encounter with Jesus. You met a man or woman—maybe at the mall or office—and you began with some small talk. Before you knew it, he or she was unraveling the entirety of your false self. What would he or she say to you? What would your response be?

2. An online medical dictionary defines *addiction* as "a persistent, compulsive dependence on a behavior or substance."[1] Discuss how that relates to Gerald May's statement "We become addicted to our own self-images."

3. "The true self is the person we can become when God is free to manifest himself through our God-given uniqueness." Does this statement confuse you, worry you, or give you hope? Why?

4. Moses was one of the most unique people in history. And yet there are many things we can relate to in his journey.

What are some aspects of his story you can relate to? Do you feel like God has a plan for you?

5. Blind spots are by definition areas that you cannot see. And we all have them. Who are the trustworthy people in your life who have permission to speak to you about your blind spots? If you don't have any such people, why?

6. "Honest worship requires the true self in right relationship with the true God." Does this ring true for you? Explain how.

Suggested prayer. Confession is an aspect of worship that we tend to downplay these days. Yet it's a significant and historical aspect of liturgical worship and the spiritual disciplines. And it's a part of the Lord's Prayer, modeled to us by Jesus himself as he taught his disciples how to pray. Confess whatever secret sins you may have to God. Ask him to reveal the depth and breadth of those sins, so you can confess fully and receive God's forgiveness. Then ask God to remind you of his unfathomable grace, which covers all sin.

CHAPTER 6: SOUL WORSHIP

1. Does John Ortberg's description of the soul—from will to mind to body—change how you see Jesus' great commandment in Matthew 22:37-38? If so, how?

2. Ortberg wrote, "Your soul is what integrates your will (your intentions), your mind (your thoughts and feelings, your values and conscience), and your body (your face, body language, and actions) into a single life. A soul is healthy—well-ordered—when there is harmony between these three

entities and God's intention for all creation." Discuss this in your group. How does alignment make sense, particularly in corporate worship?

3. Have you ever been in a worship service when you just didn't feel like worshiping? How does knowing that your will is at the center of your soul affect how you will approach this situation the next time?

4. Are you inhibited in any way in worship? Why? Are there ways in which you can work to go beyond your inhibitions?

5. What are ways in which we can further engage our intellects in worship? If you're a worship leader, how are you engaging the intellects of your congregation in worship?

6. In your own words, what does it look like not simply to participate in worship but to be a worshiper?

Suggested prayer. As a songwriter, I'm very aware that the average listener doesn't spend much time thinking about the lyrics of a song. Often it's the catchy hook that everyone focuses on. Yet we songwriters agonize over each word of our lyrics, spending days, weeks, and sometimes months on them—because lyrics really do matter. Select one of your favorite worship songs, and use the words of the song as a prayer. Beyond the melody, slowly and purposefully understand and express each lyrical phrase as a prayer to God. This exercise will increase the meaning of the song.

CHAPTER 7: WHEN THE CHURCH GATHERS

1. List half a dozen adjectives that describe the corporate personality of the church of which you're a part (for

example, friendly, informal, humorous, respectful, artistic, loud, reverent).

2. What unique traditions are shared in your community of faith? What are some of the traditions handed down to you through the church?

3. Theologian Robert Webber wrote, "Worship is a rehearsal of the saving deeds of God in history." Do you see worship primarily as an act that begins with you and God, or do you see it as a larger action into which you're invited? Does the worship you typically experience capture a sense of the grandeur of God's story? How?

4. What artistic expressions do you notice in your church? How do these acts of artistry help express your congregation's worship?

5. What are the communities of faith that you're a part of (small groups, ministry teams, families, church groups, etc.)? Are you experiencing emotional and spiritual connectedness in these communities? Why or why not?

Suggested prayer. Pray for your church. Pray for the vision and mission, pray for the elders, pastors, and staff, pray for the worship teams, the children's teachers and caregivers, the people who take care of the grounds and facilities, and the people in the pews. Pray without any agendas that God's hand would be upon your local communities of faith, upholding and sustaining them in his power and through his mercy.

CHAPTER 8: THE RHYTHM OF WORSHIP

1. Do you find it difficult to find rest? Why or why not? When was the last time you took a real Sabbath? What was it like?

2. How important is Sunday worship to you? Wouldn't miss it? Attend when you can? Or is it hit and miss? Why is that?

3. Discuss the idea that we human beings were made by God to be worshiping beings.

4. James K. A. Smith wrote, "Worship is formative, not merely expressive." Have you ever considered that worship has a spiritually formative aspect to it and that regularly scheduled worship can retune our souls?

5. Try to picture what changes would have to be made in your life and in your family in order to practice a regular Sabbath. If it seems daunting, take heart. Brainstorm just a few small changes you can enact. What would those be? Are they doable?

Suggested prayer. Pray that you would be more in touch with God's rhythm for your life, a rhythm that includes movements and prompting from the Spirit, times of quickening and slowing, and deliberate and regular times of Sabbath.

CHAPTER 9: EVERYDAY EXPRESSIONS OF WORSHIP

1. Harold Best wrote, "Worship is the continuous outpouring of all that I am, all that I do and all that I can ever become in light of a chosen or choosing [God]." Discuss this definition. In what ways are you participating in the continuous outpouring?

2. How can you increase presence (time with and attention to God)? Are there some small but doable things you can enact throughout the day? What might they be?

3. In this day and age, *obedience* seems an archaic word. Yet obedience in the small things as well as the big ones gives glory to the Father. Name some examples of ordinary acts of obedience that may be overlooked, but nevertheless please God.

4. Do you believe that God has a unique and specific purpose for you? In what ways are you stepping out in faith to be a part of God's plan, God's grand story?

5. What do you do for a living? Have you ever considered how your actions, attitudes, and performance at your place of work can be acts of worship? How does that fit into your particular scenario?

6. How does worship throughout the week affect corporate worship on Sunday? How does corporate worship on Sunday affect how you worship throughout the week?

Suggested prayer. Pray that you would become God-aware throughout the week, that your life would be more in tune with him.

CHAPTER 10: IMAGINATION AND THE WORSHIPER

1. Do you consider yourself an imaginative person? Why or why not? Give examples. (Hint: imagination is more about how you think than what you do.)

2. What do you think about the ancient idea that imagination is a part of the intellect? How might that be different from what you believe? How do you think this concept might change how you read or study the Bible?

3. What are the sacraments that are practiced in your faith tradition? What are your general experiences in practicing these sacraments?

4. Have you ever had a build-an-ark moment, a time when you had to really take a leap of faith? Explain.

5. Is imagination a value for you? For the church in which you worship? Why or why not?

Suggested prayer. Pray that God would reignite our imaginations and allow us to better see ourselves and the world as he sees.

CHAPTER 11: COMPASSION AND JUSTICE

1. Have you ever had an experience when you were moved out of your comfort zone to help another person by showing compassion and justice? What happened? How did it make you feel?

2. Have you ever associated your actions of compassion and justice with worship?

3. "Justice can be defined as a use of power in accordance with the nature of God." Discuss this definition in a group or with someone else. How may it relate, in different levels, to your personal situation?

4. "God rejects worship from hearts that don't seek right-eousness or show compassion." How does this statement affect the way you approach worship?

5. Are you currently involved in a ministry of compassion and justice? Describe your involvement to the rest of your discussion group.

6. This chapter states that the first-century church existed as an alternative community. And this is still the way we should be today. Does your local church or faith com-munity exist as an alternative community? In what ways?

Suggested prayer. In my local area, one of the more visible Christian efforts at social justice is combatting sex trafficking. Are there any organizations or ministries that are local to you? Identify a particular one, if you can, and do a little research with the goal of praying for it. Pray for the organization's vision, mission, leadership, and especially for the people it's trying to support. And you can take this one step further by actually getting involved too!

CHAPTER 12: THE DEEP END OF THE POOL

1. How would you characterize your typical worship expe-rience? Like Ezekiel, is it up to your ankles, your knees, or your waist, or is it deeper? Explain.

2. Do you have any personal trepidations about worship? Like walking into water too deep and too fast to cross, are there things—either internal or external—that keep you from fuller worship? What does this look like to you?

3. Holy fear can be defined as a deep and trembling reverence. Like the children before Aslan in *The Lion, the Witch and the Wardrobe*, we know our God is good, but he is not safe. Can the term "holy fear" be used to describe your worship experience? Is it even appropriate? Why or why not?

4. What were your expectations as you began to read this book? Were they to engage in some light reading, to gain some tips on worship, or to find some fresh perspectives? What about now?

5. When I read a book, it's not only about the content of what I'm reading, but about what God is trying to tell me through that content. What are your main takeaways from your reading?

Suggested prayer. As your final chapter prayer, simply have a time of worship in prayer. Find a quiet, alone spot, a place where you can metaphorically or physically fall on your face. Use the ACTS model for your prayer—including elements of adoration, confession, thanksgiving, and supplication (or petition).

NOTES

1 HOLY SMOKE

[1]Robert E. Webber was the first to coin the terms "blended worship" and "ancient-future" in an effort to describe the merging of worship traditions, particularly liturgical practices that focus on the story of God and modern practices that focus on emotive singing.

[2]A. W. Tozer, *A Disruptive Faith: Expect God to Interrupt Your Life* (Grand Rapids: Bethany House, 2011), 5.

[3]When I use the word *transcendence* in this context, I am not referring to the theological term, which points to God's nature as a transcendent being, distinct and above all creation (see Isaiah 55:8-9). I am referring more to the dictionary definition: existence and experience beyond the natural world.

[4]Constance M. Cherry, *The Worship Architect: A Blueprint for Designing Culturally Relevant and Biblically Faithful Services* (Grand Rapids: Baker Academic, 2010), 8.

[5]James B. Torrance, *Worship, Community, and the Triune God of Grace* (Downers Grove, IL: InterVarsity Press, 1996), 39.

[6]Gerald May, *Addiction and Grace: Love and Spirituality in the Healing of Addictions* (New York: HarperOne, 2007), 93.

2 FIRST-PERSON SINGULAR

[1]I'm not a psychologist, so I'm not trained to speak with authority on these matters. My thoughts on narcissism and other psychological matters aren't definitive but merely descriptive.

[2]Drew Pinsky and S. Mark Young, *The Mirror Effect: How Celebrity Narcissism Is Seducing America* (New York: Harper Perennial, 2010), 43-58.

[3]Pinsky and Young, *The Mirror Effect*, 89.

[4]Jean M. Twenge and W. Keith Campbell, *The Narcissism Epidemic: Living in the Age of Entitlement* (New York: Atria, 2009), 1-2.

[5]See 2 Samuel 22:4; 1 Chronicles 16:25; Psalms 18:3; 48:1; 96:4; etc. You'll find more if you do a concordance search.

[6]Rory Noland, *Worship on Earth as It Is in Heaven: Exploring Worship as a Spiritual Discipline* (Grand Rapids: Zondervan, 2011), 128.

[7]James K. A. Smith, *You Are What You Love: The Spiritual Power of Habit* (Grand Rapids: Brazos, 2016), 23.

[8]Augustine, *Confessions*, trans. R. Pine-Coffin (New York: Penguin Classics, 1961), 1.

3 FALLING ON MY FACE

[1]For more on the story of my church, Oak Hills Church in Folsom, California, please read the excellent book by my co-senior pastors, Kent Carlson and Mike Lueken, *Renovation of the Church: What Happens When a Seeker Church Discovers Spiritual Formation* (Downers Grove, IL: InterVarsity Press, 2011).

[2]C. S. Lewis, *Mere Christianity*, rev. ed. (New York: Macmillan, 1952), 109.

[3]I've told this story from A. W. Tozer a hundred times. If you know the original source, please let me know.

[4]Bruce Leafblad, "Music, Worship, and the Ministry of the Church" (lectureship presented at Western Conservative Baptist Seminary, January 1978), 47.

[5]The Levites were assigned the very important task of carrying the ark of the covenant, bringing the presence of God to the people.

4 THE NATURE OF IDENTITY

[1]Professional counseling is helpful in most cases, but also can cause damage. If you're considering getting counseling, seek a Christian counselor recommended by someone you know and trust. Be discerning but also transparent. And when you go, be as bravely and brutally honest with the counselor—and with yourself—as you can.

[2]I'm indebted to Dan Maust, a lay leader at Oak Hills Church, for providing me with his extensive notes and curriculum on spiritual transformation.

[3]Thomas Keating, *Invitation to Love: The Way of Christian Contemplation* (New York: Bloomsbury Academic, 1994), 59.

[4]"Then the eyes of both of them were opened, and they realized they were naked; so they sewed fig leaves together and made coverings for themselves" (Genesis 3:7). This is probably the first incidence of embarrassment in the history of humanity—and far from the last.

5 WORSHIP FROM THE TRUE SELF

[1]Gerald May, *Addiction and Grace: Love and Spirituality in the Healing of Addictions* (New York: HarperOne, 2007), 100.

6 SOUL WORSHIP

[1]Dallas Willard, *Renovation of the Heart: Putting on the Character of Christ* (Colorado Springs: NavPress, 2002), 32-44.

[2]Gerald May gives a tremendous and thorough description of how the neurological (body), psychological (mind), and theological (spirit) interact, as well as how God's grace provides us a way to integrated freedom. Gerald G. May, *Addiction and Grace* (New York: HarperOne, 2007).

[3]John Ortberg, *Soul Keeping: Caring for the Most Important Part of You* (Grand Rapids: Zondervan, 2004), 42-43.

[4]Note that Mark 12:30 adds "and with all your strength"; Deuteronomy 6:5, from which Jesus quoted, lists "strength" and not "mind."

[5]Bruce Leafblad, "Music, Worship, and the Ministry of the Church" (lectureship presented at Western Conservative Baptist Seminary, January 1978), 51.

[6]Willard, *Renovation of the Heart*, 41.

[7]This is the first and probably the most popular of the answers to the questions in the Westminster Catechism. The question is "What is the chief end of man?"

7 WHEN THE CHURCH GATHERS

[1]My home church, Oak Hills, is in a predominantly upper-middle-class Caucasian area in Northern California. That said, we've been very purposeful in trying to be a redemptive community that reflects diversity. For example, we've reached out to and incorporated people of color

and culture, including first- and second-generation Asians and East Indians. Almost all our ministries are intergenerational—they provide opportunities for teens and young adults up to senior citizens to minister together. Both men and women serve and minister together, from leadership (we have male and female pastors, elders, and ministry leaders) to the kitchen team and children's ministries (areas traditionally associated with women). We even have Republicans and Democrats in the same room. And we're striving toward economic diversity as well, fostering a nonjudgmental, non-class social ethic. Though we have a long way to go, such diversity is possible for us because we have a vision for being a redemptive and inclusive people. This vision is undergirded by a theology we preach from the pulpit and model to one another and the community.

[2]Robert E. Webber, *Ancient-Future Faith: Rethinking Evangelicalism for a Postmodern World* (Grand Rapids: Baker Books, 1999), 104.

[3]Robert E. Webber, *Ancient-Future Worship: Proclaiming and Enacting God's Narrative* (Grand Rapids: Baker Books, 2008), 43.

[4]Francis A. Schaeffer, *Art and the Bible* (Downers Grove, IL: InterVarsity Press, 2008), 55.

[5]At the risk of hawking myself, I cover these arguments and many others in much greater detail in my first book, *Imagine That*. In my experience, this book has helped artists of faith anchor who they are with what they do. It's a theology of the arts for dummies. Manuel Luz, *Imagine That: Discovering Your Unique Role as a Christian Artist* (Chicago: Moody Publishers, 2009).

8 THE RHYTHM OF WORSHIP

[1]Barna, "The State of the Church 2016," September 15, 2016, https://www.barna.com/research/state-church-2016.

[2]Barna, "Barna Study of Religious Change Since 1991 Shows Significant Changes by Faith Group," August 4, 2011, https://www.barna.com/research/barna-study-of-religious-change-since-1991-shows-significant-changes-by-faith-group.

[3]James K. A. Smith, *You Are What You Love: The Spiritual Power of Habit* (Grand Rapids: Brazos, 2016), 80.

9 EVERYDAY EXPRESSIONS OF WORSHIP

[1]Harold M. Best, *Unceasing Worship: Biblical Perspectives on Worship and the Arts* (Downers Grove, IL: InterVarsity Press, 2003), 18.

[2]Brother Lawrence's short book, written in the seventeenth century, is called *The Practice of the Presence of God* and is a perennial favorite.

[3]Dorothy L. Sayers, *A Matter of Eternity: Selections from the Writings of Dorothy L. Sayers* (Grand Rapids: Eerdmans, 1973), 103.

[4]There's some controversy involving the mantra-like use of breath prayers. However, I believe this is throwing the baby out with the bathwater. Rather than using breath prayers to "empty the mind," as is the goal of most Eastern practices, these short prayers are used to focus our minds toward God and away from distracting thoughts and extraneous inner self-talk.

10 IMAGINATION AND THE WORSHIPER

[1]Robert E. Webber, *Ancient-Future Worship: Proclaiming and Enacting God's Narrative* (Grand Rapids: Baker Books, 2008), 128.

[2]Dictionary.com, s.v. "imagination," 2017, www.dictionary.com/browse /imagination?s=t.

[3]Charles Sherlock, *The Doctrine of Humanity*, Contours of Christian Theology (Downers Grove, IL: IVP Academic, 1997), 78.

[4]Saint Augustine is attributed as first describing a sacrament as "an outward and visible sign of an inward and invisible grace."

[5]Andrew M. Greeley, *The Catholic Myth: The Behavior and Beliefs of American Catholics* (New York: Macmillan, 1990), 4.

11 COMPASSION AND JUSTICE

[1]Mark Labberton, *The Dangerous Act of Worship: Living God's Call to Justice* (Downers Grove, IL: InterVarsity Press, 2007), 39.

[2]Acts 2 is the definitive passage on biblical community.

[3]Although *shalom* is typically translated from the Hebrew as "peace," it has a much deeper and richer meaning than a simple lack of conflict. It implies the all-pervading will of God toward "completeness, soundness, welfare, peace" (*Strong's Exhaustive Concordance*). It's applicable to individuals, to relationships, to communities, and between

nations. Ultimately shalom comes through faith in Jesus, as Romans 5:1 declares: "Since we have been justified through faith, we have peace with God through our Lord Jesus Christ."

12 THE DEEP END OF THE POOL

[1] Annie Dillard, *Teaching a Stone to Talk* (New York: HarperCollins, 1982), 58.

DISCUSSION GUIDE

[1] The Free Dictionary, Medical Dictionary, s.v. "addiction," http://medical-dictionary.thefreedictionary.com/addiction.

ABOUT THE AUTHOR

Blog: manuelluz.com
Find resources, speaking schedule, and
thoughts on faith, worship, and the arts.

Musical instrument: walkaboutdrum.com
Manuel is the co-inventor of the
patented WalkaBout, a strap-worn
percussion instrument.

Music: iTunes or cdbaby.com

Friend him on Facebook:
facebook.com/manuelluz

formatio
TRADITION. EXPERIENCE.
TRANSFORMATION.

Formatio books from InterVarsity Press follow the rich tradition of the church in the journey of spiritual formation. These books are not merely about being informed, but about being transformed by Christ and conformed to his image. Formatio stands in InterVarsity Press's evangelical publishing tradition by integrating God's Word with spiritual practice and by prompting readers to move from inward change to outward witness. InterVarsity Press uses the chambered nautilus for Formatio, a symbol of spiritual formation because of its continual spiral journey outward as it moves from its center. We believe that each of us is made with a deep desire to be in God's presence. Formatio books help us to fulfill our deepest desires and to become our true selves in light of God's grace.